NOW
Is the Time for
MERCY

NOW
Is the Time for
MERCY

Rev. George W. Kosicki, CSB

FOREWORD BY
Fr. Joseph Roesch, MIC

REVISED EDITION

MARIAN PRESS
STOCKBRIDGE MA 01263

2010

Available from:
Marian Helpers Center
Stockbridge, MA 01263

Prayerline: 1-800-804-3823
Orderline: 1-800-462-7426
Website: www.marian.org

Imprimi Potest:
Very Rev. Daniel Cambra, MIC
Provincial Superior
The Blessed Virgin Mary, Mother of Mercy Province
September 11, 2010

Library of Congress Catalog Number: 2010935873
ISBN: 978-1-59614-232-9

Design of Cover and Pages: Kathy Szpak

Editing and Proofreading: David Came and Andrew Leeco

For texts from the English Edition of
Diary of St. Maria Faustina Kowalska

Nihil Obstat:
Lector Officialis
Most Rev. George H. Pearce, SNM

Imprimatur:
Most Rev. Joseph F. Maguire
Bishop of Springfield, Mass.
January 29, 1988

Printed in the United States of America

Sister Faustina's canonization has a particular eloquence: by this act I intend today to pass this message on to the new millennium. ...

And you, Faustina, a gift of God to our time, a gift from the land of Poland to the whole Church, obtain for us an awareness of the depth of Divine Mercy; help us to have a living experience of it and to bear witness to it among our brothers and sisters.

May your message of light and hope spread throughout the world, spurring sinners to conversion, calming rivalries and hatred, and opening individuals and nations to the practice of brotherhood. Today, fixing our gaze with you on the Face of the Risen Christ, let us make our own your prayer of trusting abandonment and say with firm hope: "Jesus, I trust in You!"

Pope John Paul II

Canonization Homily for St. Faustina,
April 30, 2000

CONTENTS

ACKNOWLEDGMENTS

We extend our special thanks to Janet Comalli and Sister Sophia Michalenko, CMGT, for typing and re-typing the manuscript and for their many helpful suggestions.

We also thank the reviewers: Father Richard Drabik, MIC, Father Donald Van Alstyne, MIC, Deacon Pete Velott, Robert Digan, Maureen Digan, James Morrison, Virginia Magdalenski, Maria Colli and Sister Dolores Liptak, RSM, who by their observations helped us to focus our text.

FOREWORD

As a member of the General Council of the Congregation of Marians, I have been granted two great privileges by God. I have had the opportunity to live in Rome for the last five years at the heart of the Church, and I have also been able to travel all over the world to visit our Marians and to help open new missions.

I was able to attend the first World Apostolic Congress on Mercy, which took place in Rome just after Divine Mercy Sunday in 2008. At the Mass in St. Peter's Square to commemorate the third anniversary of the death of Pope John Paul II (April 2, 2008), Pope Benedict XVI opened the historic Congress, stating in his homily:

> The Servant of God John Paul II had known and personally experienced the terrible tragedies of the 20th century and for a long time wondered what could stem the tide of evil. The answer could only be found in God's love. In fact, only Divine Mercy is able to impose limitations on evil; only the almighty love of God can defeat the tyranny of the wicked and the destructive power of selfishness and hate. For this reason, during his last visit to Poland, he said on his return to the land of his birth: "Apart from the mercy of God there is no other source of hope for mankind."

These are powerful words from our Holy Father of beloved memory. Human sinfulness has come close to destroying our world, but our Heavenly Father has not abandoned us. He has given us the solution in The Divine Mercy.

That World Congress in Rome in 2008 has begun a new movement of regional and diocesan Divine Mercy Congresses all over the world to teach all peoples that now, more than ever, is the time for mercy!

I had the opportunity to speak at the Asian Divine Mercy Congress, which was held in Manila in 2009. I also heard reports about some of the other regional Congresses that were held in other parts of the world.

During that trip to the Philippines, I visited a new shrine dedicated to The Divine Mercy, where our Marians began working in 2008. It is being built in El Salvador City in the Archdiocese of Cagayan de Oro in Mindanao. There is a 50-foot-tall statue of The Divine Mercy that is set on a hill over-looking the ocean. Pilgrims who visit the Shrine can climb stairways that are hidden behind the stained-glass rays of mercy. At the top of the stairs is a tiny Eucharistic Adoration chapel. There, pilgrims can adore our Lord's mercy, which is shown through His Real Presence in the Holy Eucharist.

The large statue can be seen from afar, especially when it is lit up at night. Like a lighthouse, our Lord beckons all people from near and far to come to adore and experience His great mercy.

Mindanao is a beautiful island of more than 20 million people, which is called "The Land of Promise." Sadly, parts of it have been scarred by ethnic violence and tensions for decades. Among others, priests, religious, and bishops have been kidnapped, injured, or even killed. Solutions have been sought through dialogue teams and through many government, religious, and private initiatives, but the problems persist. I am reminded of the words of our Lord to St. Faustina as recorded in her *Diary*, **Mankind will not have peace until it turns with trust to My mercy** (300).

Mercy is a concept that is meaningful to people of many different faiths. In our Christian understanding of mercy, we speak not just of a concept or an attribute but also of a person — Jesus Christ, who is The Divine Mercy Incarnate. He came to the world to reveal the merciful face of His Father. In the Sermon on the Mount, He taught us, "Blessed are the merciful, for they will be shown mercy" (Mt 5:7).

The Divine Mercy message, which was revealed to St. Faustina just before World War II, was given to remind us of these Gospel truths that we have forgotten. A Marian Father, Fr. Joseph Jarzebowski, MIC, brought the message to the United States in 1941 after he had received it from St. Faustina's confessor and spiritual director, Fr. Michael Sopocko (who was beatified in 2008). A ban on the message and devotion according to the forms revealed to St. Faustina occurred in 1959 because of poor translations and because of the political situation in Poland. It slowed down the dissemination of the message for nearly 20 years. However, the lifting of the ban by the Church in 1978 and then the publication of the *Diary of St. Faustina* in the 1980s brought a veritable explosion in the dissemination of this message.

In this wonderful book, *Now Is the Time for Mercy*, Fr. George Kosicki, CSB, and his coauthor, Vinny Flynn, tell us the basics of this timely and life-changing message. This revised edition of the book, along with some updating, includes new material on trust at the beginning of Part I: The Message of Divine Mercy. Further, the Chronology of Events at the end of the book has been revised and expanded to reflect new developments in the spread of the message.

Now Is the Time for Mercy was first published in the early 1990s. The 1990s was a difficult decade marked by violence of many kinds, including the Oklahoma City bombing in 1995 and the Columbine High School massacre in 1999.

The new millennium has witnessed a host of new problems that remind us the message of the Divine Mercy is more urgent than ever. The tragedy of September 11, 2001, is seared in the memory of all who lived through it. The threat of global terrorism continues to this day. In our society at large, we are witnessing moral confusion and growing secularism. Pope Benedict has reminded us that our Church as well is in need of reform and renewal in light of the recent clergy sexual abuse scandals. Emphasizing the need for forgiveness and mercy, he closed the Year for Priests on June 11, 2010, saying that the very fact the scandals had been highlighted during the special year should be considered "as a summons to purification" for the Church. Then, there was the tragic oil spill that couldn't be easily stopped in the Gulf of Mexico, starting in the spring of 2010, which seems to symbolize the mess we find ourselves in.

In light of all these problems, where can we turn but to the mercy of God? One year after the death of John Paul II, Pope Benedict reminded the world on Divine Mercy Sunday in 2006 that "Divine Mercy is not a secondary devotion but an integral dimension of Christian faith and prayer." The faithful had already been living the truth of these words. In the last several decades, The Divine Mercy message and devotion has become one of the fastest growing grassroots movements in the history of the Church. And as a result of the Divine Mercy Congresses mentioned earlier, this message is now being celebrated not only at a grassroots level but also at the heart of the Church.

On April 30, 2000, Pope John Paul II canonized St. Faustina Kowalska as the first Saint of the Great Jubilee Year of the Incarnation. During his homily that day, Pope John Paul stated:

> Sister Faustina's canonization has a particular eloquence. By this act, I intend today to pass this message on to the new millennium. I pass it on to all people, so that they will learn to know ever better the true face of God and the true face of their brethren.

Pope John Paul II worked tirelessly to prepare the world for the Great Jubilee in honor of the birth of our Savior. He then lived to see five years of the new millennium. The Venerable Servant of God realized that the world would need to experience God's mercy today more than ever.

Perhaps that is why on the same day as St. Faustina's canonization, he declared, "It is important then that we accept the whole message that comes to us from the word of God on this Second Sunday of Easter, which from now on throughout the Church will be called 'Divine Mercy Sunday.'" Perhaps only in heaven will we learn how important this gesture was on the part of Pope John Paul II in establishing Divine Mercy Sunday as a universal feast day. Only God is aware of all of the graces that have been poured out on the world through the annual celebrations in honor of The Divine Mercy.

As you learn about this important message through reading this book, I trust that you will not only be enriched by it but that your life will be changed as well. May you take this message to heart and begin to live it.

Fr. Joseph Roesch, MIC
Zakopane, Poland
June 21, 2010

PREFACE

In a scene from the film *Divine Mercy — No Escape*, Fr. John Bertolucci explains that "what God really wants us to know through St. Faustina ... is the truth that He is Mercy ... and the greatest thing for us is to be merciful."

"God is Mercy." What does that really mean? What is mercy? And what does it really have to do with us in our daily lives?

These are the kinds of questions that this book attempts to answer as it presents a series of teachings on mercy, leading us further into the message of The Divine Mercy devotion.

Here, the meaning of mercy and the urgency of the message can be pondered in the words of Sacred Scripture, in the words of Pope John Paul II, and in the words of our Lord to St. Faustina of Poland during the 1930s (as recorded in her *Diary*).

In the Appendix, we have included reflections on the "Importance of Private Revelations" and a "Chronology of Events" related to the message and devotion to The Divine Mercy. We have also included three studies that we call "Toward a Theology of — the Image, the Chaplet, and the Feast," which begin to open up the rich significance of these three elements of The Divine Mercy message.

Through this and other books on Divine Mercy, the message can be read and re-read and allowed to touch our hearts profoundly, helping us to fulfill in our daily lives the gospel command of Christ:

"Be merciful, even as your Father is merciful" (Lk 6:36 RSV).

INTRODUCTION

Our Lord's revelations to St. Faustina speak of *now* as the *time of mercy*. There is a special urgency in this message. Repeatedly, our Lord stressed that *now* is the day of mercy before the coming of the day of judgment. *Now* is the time to prepare for the coming of the Lord. "Write this," He said to her:

> **Before I come as the Just Judge, I am coming first as the King of Mercy** (*Diary*, 83).
>
> **I am prolonging the time of mercy for the sake of** [sinners]**. But woe to them if they do not recognize this time of My visitation** (*Diary*, 1160).

To this powerful message from the Lord, St. Faustina adds her own exhortation. "O human souls," she asks, "where are you going to hide on the day of God's anger? Take refuge now in the fount of God's mercy" (*Diary*, 848).

We find a strong sense of this urgency in the writings of Pope John Paul II, who as the Archbishop of Krakow initiated the cause for the beatification of St. Faustina. He was instrumental in having the studies prepared that, on April 15, 1978, led to the complete removal of the 20-year ban on the devotion. Six months later to the day, he was elected Bishop of Rome! In his encyclical *Rich in Mercy*, he cites "lack of peace" in our hearts and in the world as the problem of our times — a problem which can only be answered by God's mercy. His encyclical is a strong summons for us to implore mercy for ourselves and for the whole world — *now*.

> In the name of Jesus Christ crucified and risen from the dead, in the spirit of his messianic mission, which endures in the works of mankind, we lift up our voice and plead: that the love which is in the Father may once again be revealed at this stage of history and that, through the work of The Son and The Holy Spirit, that

may be shown to be present in our modern world and be shown to be more powerful than evil: more powerful than sin and death (*Rich in Mercy*).

Of the 6.8 billion people in the world, 14 million are Jewish, 1.5 billion are Muslim, and 2.1 billion are Christian, of which 1.1 billion are Catholics. This leaves some 3.2 billion who do not even know that there is a merciful God, and many more who are refusing to trust in His mercy.

In the face of this situation, our Lord's words to us through St. Faustina are unmistakably clear:

> **Speak to the world about My mercy: let all mankind recognize My unfathomable mercy. It is a sign for the end times; after it will come the day of justice. While there is still time, let them have recourse to the fount of My mercy; let them profit from the Blood and Water which gushed forth for them** (*Diary*, 848).

So, the challenge awaits us *now* to speak out and tell the world of this infinitely merciful God who is waiting for us to turn to Him with trust and become merciful to others as He is merciful to us.

It is our hope and prayer that this book will be the catalyst for a worldwide response to God's mercy as presented to us through St. Faustina.

> God's floodgates have been opened for us. Let us want to take advantage of them before the day of God's justice arrives (*Diary*, 1159).

> O what a great multitude of souls I see! They worshiped The Divine Mercy and will be singing the hymn of praise for all eternity (*Diary*, 848).

PART I
The Message of Divine Mercy

When fears of unknown or known origin, anxieties and confusion, and resentments all converge at once, we can easily ask ourselves this question. "What is it all about?" Then, add to it worries over family and finances. Mix in strained relations with those at work and frustration with our jobs. Finally, top it off with sickness. It is then that we scream, "Lord, what is it all about? Help! Mercy!"

It is precisely, then, that we need to try to listen to the silent voice of God deep within our hearts, pleading with us, crying out like a voice in the desert, "Trust Me!" God speaks very loudly, but His language is usually silence (see *Diary*, 888). Once our hearts are stilled, His most common words to us are: "Do not be afraid. I am with you. Trust Me." This message is often found in the Sacred Scriptures, because it is so fundamental to our human predicament. Consider this verse from the Psalms: "Trust God at all times, my people! Pour out your hearts to God our refuge!" (Ps 62:9).

IT'S ALL ABOUT TRUST

Trust in the Lord is *what it is all about*. Trust is the humble and free exercise of our free will, submitting our will to the will of God. It is our faith, hope, and love put into action in responding to God's great mercy. Trust is a concrete and practical way to practice humility.

It calls us to rely on God as the giver of all good gifts and the provider of all our needs. Trust is a way to proclaim the truth that God is my Creator and Redeemer who cares for me.

The powerful prayer of the heart "Jesus, I trust in You!" is our basic response to the question: "What's it all about?" It's all about trusting in Jesus, who is the Way, the Truth and the Life. In proclaiming "Jesus, I trust in You," I proclaim Jesus as the source of all grace and light in the midst of my darkness. This proclamation helps clear the cloud of fears and anxieties within and around me. It is a battle cry that pierces the gloom, drawing our attention to the victory already won in heaven by Jesus, so that the victory may be ours on earth.

The cry of "Jesus, I trust in You" is an effective plea for the coming of the kingdom where Jesus reigns, to the glory of the Father. It is a cry of victory over the works of the Evil One. Our profession "Jesus, I trust in You" proclaims to our God that "the kingdom, the power, and the glory are Yours now and forever. Amen."

Turning to the imagery of St. Faustina, trust in the Lord opens the floodgates of God's mercy upon us. God just can't resist the humble, trusting soul, and He floods it with His love and mercy. We learn this time and again in the *Diary*.

Repeatedly, in His conversations with Sister Faustina, the Lord spoke of His merciful response to souls that trust in Him: **I desire to grant unimaginable graces, He told her, to those souls who trust in My mercy. ... Sooner would heaven and earth turn into nothingness than would My mercy not embrace a trusting soul** (*Diary*, 687, 1777).

Over and over again, He stressed that He could never reject a repentant heart, never refuse an appeal to His mercy:

> **I am Mercy itself for the contrite soul. ... Souls that make an appeal to My mercy delight me. To such souls, I grant even more graces than they ask. I cannot punish even the greatest sinner if he makes an appeal to My compassion** (*Diary*, 1739, 1146).

THE GIFT OF GOD'S PEACE

In His conversations with Sister Faustina, The Lord emphasized the connection between turning to His mercy and finding peace:

> **The flames of mercy are burning Me. I desire to pour them out upon human souls. Oh, what pain they cause Me when they do not want to accept them!**

> **My daughter, do whatever is within your power to spread devotion to My mercy. I will make up for what you lack. Tell aching mankind to snuggle close to My merciful Heart, and I will fill it with peace** (*Diary*, 1074).

This is the peace of the Lord that we so desperately need in our lives when we are troubled or agitated. But this peace that comes from trusting in God's mercy isn't just for us individually. No, it is also for nations and the whole world. The path to peace is not found in summit meetings, stockpiling arms, or in acquiring more material goods. The path to peace is found only in trusting in God's mercy for our lives. Our Lord makes this quite clear through His powerful words to Sister Faustina: **Mankind will not have peace until it turns with trust to My mercy** (*Diary*, 300).

So, what's it all about?

Trust!

SOME TIPS FOR GROWING IN TRUST

To grow in trust, especially when you are in difficulty, try repeating over and over again, from the heart: "Jesus, I trust in You!" Make it a cry of the heart to the Lord in your immediate need. Be mindful that Jesus is The Divine Mercy Incarnate — the One who stands at the door of our hearts, waiting for us to open them even a little bit (see Rev 3:20 and *Diary*, 1486, 1507). Then, He, in his great mercy, will do the rest.

We can also be mindful that we are called to sign the image of The Divine Mercy with the words "Jesus, I trust in You!" This image of Jesus is a vessel with which we are to keep coming to Him for graces in our need (see *Diary*, 327). So, in quiet moments throughout your day, gaze upon the image of the Merciful Savior. Carry the image with you on a prayer card, which you can keep in your wallet or purse. Frame a print of the image and place it in your home and office. Look for a decal or magnet, so you can display it on the fridge or the dashboard of your car. Further, look for an image of The Divine Mercy that you can use as a screensaver on your computer.

Here's another tip: In the midst of the battle, shout the victory cheer: T.R.U.S.T.

Total
Reliance
Upon
Saving
Truth

TRUST IN JESUS AND DESIRE FOR SAINTHOOD

As we grow in trusting the Lord, the greatest desire of our heart should be the call to sainthood. Our desire is to live forever with Jesus in heaven and to do His will during our life here on earth. This is the universal call to holiness for all baptized Christians. It is the strong and clear mandate given in the *Dogmatic Constitution on the Church*, one of the main documents of the Second Vatican Council.

We have seen in Faustina's great desire to be a saint the fulfillment of this mandate. By canonizing her, the Church has established her as a model of sanctity for all of us. The central message of St. Faustina's life is her complete trust in Jesus. Her great trust enabled her to attain her goal of sainthood. In her *Diary*, she teaches us that the desire for holiness, when combined with complete trust in God's mercy, makes sainthood accessible to all of us. All God needs is "a bit of good will" from us. Then, He will do the rest:

> O my Jesus, how very easy it is to become holy; all that is needed is a bit of good will. If Jesus sees this little bit of good will in the soul, He hurries to give Himself to the soul, and nothing can stop Him, neither shortcomings nor falls — absolutely nothing. Jesus is anxious to help that soul, and if it is faithful to this grace from God, it can very soon attain the highest holiness possible for a creature here on earth. God is very generous and does not deny His grace to anyone. Indeed He gives more than what we ask of Him (*Diary*, 291).

In another passage, Jesus tells us that even "the greatest sinners" could achieve great holiness if only they would trust in His mercy:

> **My dearest secretary, write that I want to pour out My divine life into human souls and to sanctify them, if only they were willing to accept My grace. The greatest sinners would achieve great sanctity, if only they would trust in My mercy** (*Diary*, 1784).

PERSEVERANCE

We are called to persevere in our trust in the Lord, especially when we suffer or face setbacks in life. Whether the anguish was physical or spiritual, Faustina continued to trust and embrace suffering in the spirit of Jesus. The Lord told her: **Both the sinner and the righteous person have need of**

My mercy. Conversion, as well as perseverance, is a grace of My mercy (*Diary*, 1577).

Our perseverance is based on our trust in the Lord and His provision for us. After all, everything that the merciful God has arranged for us to experience at every moment is the best and holiest thing possible. Therefore, we should rejoice and give thanks, with an active abandonment to God's will, not just a passive submission. In that spirit, we then do the best we can in each and every vicissitude. As we do this, we can entrust all our concerns to the merciful Heart of Jesus and to the Immaculate Heart of Mary, Mother of Mercy.

WHAT IS MERCY?

Now that we understand the importance of trust, we can consider the meaning of mercy in God's plan. The message of Divine Mercy is that God is merciful. He is love itself poured out for us, and He wants no one to escape that merciful love.

The message is that God wants us to turn to Him with trust and repentance while it is still a time of mercy — before He comes as the Just Judge — a time of mercy that is a preparation for His Second Coming.

This turning with trust to Him who is mercy itself is the only source of peace for mankind, the only answer to the troubled world — there is no escaping that answer.

The message of Divine Mercy is not something new. It is the message of the gospel, the message of the Church throughout the ages, the message of Pope John Paul II in his encyclical *Rich in Mercy*, the message of our Lord through St. Faustina. It is all one consistent message of mercy.

If we want to understand more clearly what mercy is and what it means to be merciful, it helps to use two words: *merciful* and *merciflow*.

God's love has been poured into our hearts through
the Holy Spirit (Rom 5:5 RSV).

In the Trinity, the love that is God is a constantly flowing,
creative power. From the love of the Father proceeds the Son,
and from the love of the Father and Son together proceeds the
Holy Spirit (see *The Credo*). As this love flows outward from the
Trinity and, through the action of the Holy Spirit, pours itself
out in creation and redemption, it becomes mercy.

Mercy, then, is God's love poured out upon us; it is
when God, who is Love itself, loves us.

This flowing quality of mercy is most dramatically represented by Christ on the cross as, through the blood and water
gushing forth from His pierced Heart, He pours His very life
out as a fountain of mercy for us. It is represented, too, in the
Eucharist as, under the appearances of bread and wine, Christ
continues to pour Himself into our hearts. And we also find it in
the great chant of the Church, the "Kyrie Eleison" (Lord, have
mercy), which for centuries has resounded throughout the
world at every celebration of the Eucharist and Liturgy of the
Hours. The word *eleison*, which is Greek means "have mercy,"
has the root meaning of "oil being poured out." So, whenever
we say, "Lord, have mercy," we are really saying, "Lord, pour
Your love out upon us, pour *Yourself* out upon us."

This outpoured love is the essence of the priesthood of
Christ, a priesthood based on a covenant of mercy. As High
Priest, Christ brought God's gift of mercy to man — bringing
forgiveness of sin by the sacrifice of His own Body and Blood on
the cross — as a new and eternal covenant of God's merciful love.

Moreover, God has willed to take us into partnership in
this work of mercy. By our Baptism, we are partners of Christ,
the one High Priest, Redeemer and Mediator. Like Mary, the
Mother of God and of the Church, we too are cooperators
with Christ in the work of redemption and mediation; in this
work of mercy, we are channels of mercy to others.

As the mercy of God flows into us, it cleanses us,
converts us, turns us around, so that we, too, can become

merciful (and merciflow). Filled with mercy ourselves, we allow that mercy to flow through us — toward God in thanksgiving and praise, and toward our neighbor in love and works of mercy. In turn, the mercy that flows through us to God and our neighbor flows back to us, fulfilling the scriptural promise, "Blessed are the merciful, for they shall obtain mercy" (Mt 5:7 RSV). They let mercy flow.

SCRIPTURAL APPROACH

In the film, *Divine Mercy — No Escape*, Rabbi Kushner of the Temple Israel in Natick, Massachusetts, gives us a wonderful insight into the meaning of this word mercy, a wonderful description of the way God loves us, and thus, the way we should love each other:

> The God of the Hebrew Bible is a God of mercy, a God of forgiveness. "For I desire not the death of the sinner but that he turn from his evil ways and return to me." When the Hebrew people first meet God, He is in the process of freeing them from slavery in Egypt — not because they had earned their freedom, but because He loved them and wanted them to be free.
>
> There are two words for mercy in the Hebrew Bible: *hesed*, which means giving people more than they deserve, going beyond strict justice; and *rachamim*, which is the love a mother feels for her child, enabling her to say, "I hope you will be worthy, but whether you are or not, you and I belong to each other in an intimacy that nothing can ever change." God loves us that way, and if we human beings are fashioned in the image of God, it doesn't mean that God looks like us — brown hair and slightly overweight — but that we have qualities of the soul that God has, and that no other living [material] creatures share with Him — including the gift of being merciful as He is merciful.

We can build on what Rabbi Kushner said about mercy by expanding the description of the word *hesed*, and thus come to the richness of the word in Hebrew and its importance to us.

The Hebrew word *hesed* (mercy) according to John L. McKenzie in the *Dictionary of the Bible*, is most clearly seen by studying the words with which it is associated. *Hesed*, commonly associated with *emet* (steadfastness), means that God is faithful and dependable and so worthy of our trust. *Hesed* with *sedakah* (righteousness) means that God reveals Himself as righteous to the upright. *Hesed* with *yesua* (salvation) is seen as the will to save and is similar to *hesed* associated with *shalom* (peace). *Hesed* with *rachamim* (motherly tenderness) reveals God's tender pity toward those who are in misery.

But most frequently, *hesed* is associated with covenant. God's continued *hesed* with Israel depended on their fidelity to His commandments. The *covenant* itself is called *hesed*, and preserves and demonstrates mercy. The *hesed* of covenant is why the Israelites could appeal to God for forgiveness in their infidelity — because God is faithful and merciful. The covenant arises from God's sovereign action — His initiative and His election of Israel:

> The entire history of the dealing of Yahweh with Israel can be summed up as *hesed*; it is the dominating motive which appears in His deeds and the motive which gives unity and intelligibility to all His dealings with men, including such things as anger and judgment (J. L. McKenzie).

In the New Testament — the *New Covenant* — God acts sovereignly by His initiative and His election to have mercy on all (see Rm 11:32). Out of His infinite merciful love, God sends His Son to reveal His mercy. Jesus reveals "God, who is rich in mercy" as Father (see Eph 2:4 and *Rich in Mercy*, 1). Jesus, then, sets the goal of our lives:

> Be merciful, even as your Father is merciful (Lk 6:36 RSV).

In the New Testament, the Greek word *eleo* (mercy) is used for the Hebrew *hesed*. The word eleo carries with it the attitude of Christ, who is ready to associate with sinners and ready to forgive. In Christ, *eleo* (mercy) initiates and completes the process of salvation. In men, it comes very close to *agape* (love) as seen in the readiness to forgive. In the New Testament, *eleo* between men is transformed by love, which is a revolutionary development, and places a deeper motivation behind *eleo* than we find in the Old Testament (adapted from J. L. McKenzie).

Unfortunately, the one English word "mercy" does not carry the meaning of h*esed* and *eleo*. The Latin word *misericordia* literally means the compassion of the heart. The Polish word *milosierdzie* means love of the heart. There is no one single English word which is adequate to carry the full meaning, so a combination of words are used; such as, loving kindness, heartfelt love, merciful love, faithful love, steadfast love.

THE GREATEST ATTRIBUTE OF GOD

Through the Scriptures, the word *mercy* is so identified with God that in understanding mercy we come to understand something of God's character.

Mercy, explains Pope John Paul II, is the "most stupendous attribute" of God! It reveals to us what God is like. It is "love's second name":

God, who is love, reveals Himself to us as mercy.

The Bible, tradition and the whole faith life of the People of God provide unique proof ... that mercy is the greatest of the attributes and perfections of God (John Paul II, *Rich in Mercy*, 14).

Saint Faustina also came to realize that God's plan of merciful love is the revelation of His greatest attribute:

I understood that the greatest attribute is love and mercy. It unites the creature with the Creator. This immense love and abyss of mercy are made known in the Incarnation of the Word and in the Redemption [of humanity], and it is here that I saw this as the greatest of all God's attributes (*Diary*, 180).

MERCY IS LOVE POURED THROUGH THE PIERCED HEART OF JESUS

The pierced Heart of Christ crucified is the convergence point of all events, time, and love. It is like a converging lens, bringing together in one point the fullness of God's love poured out for us. This love then comes forth as mercy — a flood of His blood and water as a fount of mercy for us. Mercy is love poured through the pierced Heart of Jesus.

The focusing lens, the lens that points and gathers all things to the pierced Heart of Jesus, is the Immaculate Heart of Mary. In Mary's Heart we are focused on the Heart of Jesus.

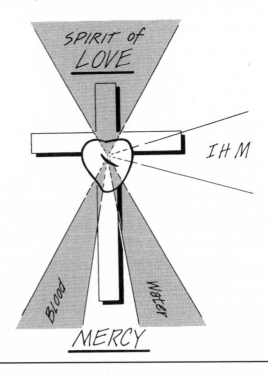

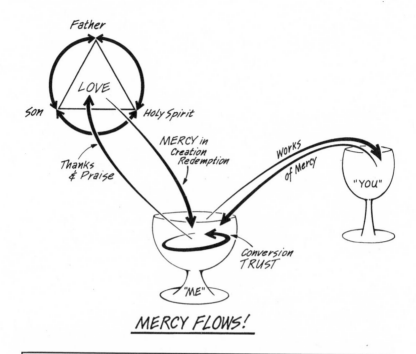

MERCY FLOWS!

Mercy	is love's second name.
Mercy	is infinite because it is the perfection of the infinite God.
Mercy	flows from meditation on the word of God, from the Eucharist which is love greater than death, and from Reconciliation which is love greater than sin.
Mercy	is revealed in Christ crucified and risen which is love greater than death, sin, and evil.
Mercy	is the program and mission of the Church because it is the program and mission of Christ.
Mercy	is the content and power of the Gospel.
Mercy	is centered in the Heart of Jesus and continued in the Heart of Mary.

Adapted from John Paul II,
Rich in Mercy

WHO RECEIVES MERCY?

God shows you generous patience, since He wants none to perish, but all to come to repentance (2 Pet 3:9 NAB).

God wants to have mercy on all; He wants no one to escape from His mercy, because it is only through His mercy that we are saved. We do not merit or earn salvation by our good works and efforts. It is all a gift. The Father invites us all to turn to Jesus, who is Mercy Incarnate, as the source of salvation. "I am the way, the truth, and the life," Jesus tells us, "and no one comes to the Father, but by Me" (Jn 14:6 RSV).

Jesus, The Divine Mercy, is the only way to salvation, and God wants no one to escape from that way. But this plan of His has God, in a human way of speaking, in a "dilemma." He loves us and wants to possess us, by absorbing us into that love so that we can rejoice with Him forever; but He has created us free and so must allow us to accept His merciful love freely. So He pursues us in countless ways, patiently waiting for us to turn to Him and freely accept the gift of His love.

If, in spite of His efforts, we do not freely open up to Him then He allows us to suffer for a time in our sinfulness, allows us to be shaken, broken open, even crushed by the events of our lives, until finally, we cry, "Mercy!" In this way, His plan is fulfilled; we've cried for mercy, and so He can have mercy on us.

In a way, God is like a frustrated lover, pleading for us to open our hearts to Him and allow Him to do what He so delights in doing — having mercy on us and possessing us with His love. He wants no one to escape His Mercy.

St. Paul, in writing to the Church in Rome, summarizes in one verse this plan of God for Israel and the Church: "God has imprisoned all in disobedience," he writes, "so that He might have mercy on all" (Rom 11:32 NAB).

In our own times, through a series of revelations to St. Faustina Kowalska of Poland during the 1930s, our Lord has asked us to proclaim His mercy and to offer the sacrifice of mercy for others. His main message was the urgent need for people to turn to His compassionate heart, trusting Him, accepting His mercy, and offering that same mercy to others by prayer, words, and deeds.

The Lord shared with St. Faustina His burning desire to pour out His mercy upon us all, and He pleaded for us to draw upon His mercy while it was still the time of mercy, before His coming as just judge. He repeatedly spoke of the immensity of His mercy, and of His merciful love for all, especially great sinners and those in misery:

> **My Secretary, write that I am more generous toward sinners than toward the just. It was for their sake that I came down from heaven; it was for their sake that My Blood was spilled. Let them not fear to approach Me; they are most in need of My mercy** (*Diary*, 1275).

The more miserable a soul is, He explained to her, the more it has a right to His mercy. His mercy is like a vast, bottomless ocean, while our sin is but a drop of water. It is greater than all our sins, all our fears, all our anxieties, all our darkness and depression. And it is available for everyone:

> [Urge] **all souls to trust in the unfathomable abyss of My mercy, because I want to save them all. On the cross, the fountain of My mercy was opened wide by the lance for all souls — no one have I excluded!** (*Diary*, 1182).

God's mercy is always available, because His plan and desire is to have mercy on us all. He wants no one to escape from His Merciful Heart.

Because of our free will, we can frustrate His plan by not accepting His love. God's mercy is like the sun. It is always shining on us, but we can choose to escape its warmth and light by hiding in the cold darkness of our own caves. God is always loving us, and we can't change that. He loves us, no matter what we do, and is always ready to forgive; so, in that sense we can never escape the reality of His mercy.

But, unfortunately, we can reject it. We can continue to the very end in rejecting God's great mercy, refusing to accept the love and forgiveness He offers us, resisting His constant efforts to bring us back to Him.

For those who thus choose God's justice instead of the mercy He longs to bestow, the words *no escape* take on a different meaning. They have escaped His mercy by refusing to accept it, and for them, there will be no escape from His justice, no escape from their self-imposed prison of sin and darkness:

> **Tell sinners that no one shall escape My Hand; if they run away from My Merciful Heart, they will fall into My Just Hands** (*Diary*, 1728).

In one section of her *Diary*, St. Faustina records a conversation between our merciful God and a despairing sinner, showing how continuously and lovingly God offers forgiveness, while still respecting the final, free-will choice of the individual soul:

> Jesus: **O soul steeped in darkness, do not despair. All is not yet lost. Come and confide in your God, who is love and mercy.**
> — But the soul, deaf even to this appeal, wraps itself in darkness.
> Jesus calls out again: **My child, listen to the voice of your merciful Father**.
> In the soul arises this reply: "For me there is no mercy," and it falls into greater darkness, a despair which is a foretaste of hell and makes it unable to draw near to God.

Jesus calls to the soul a third time, but the soul remains deaf and blind, hardened and despairing. The mercy of God begins to exert itself, and, without any cooperation from the soul, God grants it final grace. If this too is spurned, God will leave the soul in this self-chosen disposition for eternity. This grace emerges from the merciful Heart of Jesus and gives the soul a special light by means of which the soul begins to understand God's effort; but conversion depends on its own will. The soul knows that this, for her, is final grace and, should it show even a flicker of good will, the mercy of God will accomplish the rest (*Diary*, 1486).

The Good Samaritan — A Parable of Mercy
(Lk 10:29-37).

To a lawyer who asked Him, "And who is my neighbor?" Jesus responded with the parable of the Good Samaritan, ending the parable with the exhortation, "Go and do likewise." The usual interpretation is that we ought to be good Samaritans when we see our brother in need. And this is right; we must be merciful to those in misery.

There is, however, another way to interpret the message of the parable, and that is to identify ourselves with the poor man who had been robbed, stripped, and beaten up. We are the poor miserable ones left on the side of the road, half dead. Jesus is the Good Samaritan who comes along as our Savior to bind up our wounds, pouring oil and wine on them, and bearing us to the place of rest where He takes care of us and pays the price for all our needs.

This is Mercy! Jesus has reached out to us while we were still sinners and laid down His life for us (see Rm 5:6-8). Jesus has washed us clean through the water of Baptism, anointing us with His Holy Spirit, feeding us with His own Body and Blood, bringing us home into His body, the Church. All of this love through no merit of our own. That is Divine Mercy — and He wants no one to escape from that Mercy!

HOW DO WE RECEIVE MERCY?

I stand at the door and knock.
If anyone hears My voice and opens the door,
I will come in to him and eat with him
And he with Me (Rv 3:20 RSV).

"A flicker of good will" is all God's mercy requires in order to bring even the worst of sinners to final repentance. Our Merciful Savior stands patiently before the doors of our hearts, calling to us. All we need to do is respond to His love. At one point, He said to St. Faustina:

> Let no one doubt concerning the goodness of God; even if a person's sins were as dark as night, God's mercy is stronger than our misery. One thing alone is necessary: that the sinner set ajar the door of his heart, be it ever so little, to let in the ray of God's merciful grace, and then God will do the rest (*Diary*, 1507).

Just what does it mean to "set ajar" the doors of our hearts and thus receive the Lord's mercy? As our opening section showed us, the answer is *Trust:*

> **The graces of My Mercy are drawn by means of one vessel only, and that is — trust. The more a soul trusts, the more it will receive. Souls that trust boundlessly are a great comfort to Me, because I pour all the treasures of My graces into them** (*Diary*, 1578).

Repeatedly, in His conversations with St. Faustina, the Lord spoke of His merciful response to souls who trust in Him. **I desire to grant unimaginable graces to those souls who trust in My Mercy** (*Diary*, 687).

Sooner would heaven and earth turn into nothingness than would My mercy not embrace a trusting soul (*Diary*, 1777).

Over and over again He stressed that He could never reject a repentant heart, never refuse an appeal to His mercy:

> I am Mercy itself for the contrite soul (*Diary*, 1739). Souls that make an appeal to My mercy delight Me. To such souls I grant even more graces than they ask. I cannot punish even the greatest sinner if he makes an appeal to My compassion ... (*Diary*, 1146).

"*Jesus, I trust in You!*" says it all. When we call on the name of Jesus, we acknowledge that He is our Savior and Lord. This short prayer capsulizes the devotion to The Divine Mercy. Jesus wants to have mercy on all. He is being consumed by the flames of this desire, but the only ones upon whom He can pour out His mercy are those who trust in Him:

> I want to pour out My divine life into human souls and to sanctify them, if only they were willing to accept My grace. The greatest sinners would achieve great sanctity, if only they would trust in My mercy. The very inner depths of My being are filled to overflowing with mercy, and it is being poured out upon all I have created (*Diary*, 1784).

In His conversations with St. Faustina, The Lord also emphasized the connection between trusting in Him and finding peace:

> The flames of mercy are burning Me. I desire to pour them out upon human souls. Oh, what pain they cause Me when they do not want to accept them!
>
> My daughter, do whatever is within your power to spread devotion to My mercy. I will make up for

what you lack. Tell aching mankind to snuggle close to My merciful Heart, and I will fill it with peace (*Diary*, 1074).

The Prodigal Son — A Parable of Mercy
(Lk 15:11-32)

Jesus told us the great parable of mercy without even using the word "mercy." It is the parable of the Father with two sons. The younger son asked for his share of the inheritance, and then went off and spent it all in loose living. When he had spent everything, a great famine struck the country, and he was in dire need. In his misery, he even went so far as to work for a farmer feeding pigs, and he was so hungry that he wanted to eat the fodder, himself.

Then, coming to his senses, he realized that back in his father's house, even the servants had enough to eat. So, he decided to go back to his father's house, confess his sin and ask to be treated as a hired hand, because he was no longer worthy to be called a son.

But the father, keeping watch, sees him coming home, and has different plans. Filled with compassion, he runs to greet him, and orders a celebration for his son, who was dead, and now alive; lost, and now found.

The father also reaches out with mercy to his elder son. Ignoring his envy and anger the father explains that he is always with his son and all that he has as father belongs to him as son. The father reaches out even further and challenges the son to be merciful and rejoice because his younger brother is alive.

The father is merciful toward both of his sons, because he loves them both, and they both need mercy. The mercy of the father restores his own fatherhood and the sonship of his younger son. In reaching out to the elder, self-righteous son, the father shows mercy to him as well.

Whether we are like the younger or like the elder son — or a mixture of both — our Heavenly Father wants to have mercy on all of us, if we let Him, by our trusting Him.

HOW DO WE GIVE MERCY?

Be merciful as your Father in heaven is merciful (Lk 6:36 RSV).

As Christians, we are called to be merciful to others in the same way God the Father is merciful to us. In a word, we are to love our neighbor as God has loved us.

Our Lord explained to St. Faustina that faith alone would not suffice. **There must also be acts of mercy ... even the strongest faith will be of no use without works** (*Diary*, 742).

> **I am giving you three ways of exercising mercy toward your neighbor: the first — by deed, the second — by word, the third — by prayer. In these three degrees is contained the fullness of mercy, and it is an unquestionable proof of love for Me. By this means a soul glorifies and pays reverence to My mercy.** (*Diary*, 742).

These, then, must become our fundamental way of expressing trust in the mercy of God, By deeds of mercy, we show others how to be merciful; by our words of encouragement and advice, in preaching, teaching, and writing, we let others know of God's mercy; by prayer, we implore mercy for sinners and glorify the mercy of the Lord.

The Church has taught the works of mercy in two groups: the Corporal and Spiritual Works of Mercy. The Corporal Works of Mercy are feeding the hungry, giving drink to the thirsty, clothing the naked, sheltering the travelers, comforting the prisoners, visiting the sick, and burying the dead. The Spiritual Works of Mercy include teaching the ignorant, praying for the living and the dead, correcting sinners, counseling those in doubt, consoling the sorrowful, bearing wrongs patiently, and forgiving wrongs willingly.

For those who feel that these works are too dramatic, too removed from the situations we "ordinary" people encounter in our daily lives, Blessed Mother Teresa offered an explanation that suggests the countless opportunities we all have to be channels of His mercy:

> Jesus says, "Whatever you do to the least of your brothers is done in My name. When you receive a little child you receive Me. If in My name you give a glass of water, you give it to Me." And to make sure that we understand what He is talking about, He says that at the hour of death we are going to be judged only that way. I was hungry, you gave Me to eat. I was naked, you clothed Me. I was homeless, you took Me in. Hunger is not only for bread; hunger is for love. Nakedness is not only for a piece of clothing; nakedness is lack of human dignity, and also that beautiful virtue of purity, and lack of respect for each other. Homelessness is not only being without a home made of bricks; homelessness is also being rejected, unwanted, unloved (*Jesus, the Word to be Spoken*, Servant Books, Ann Arbor, MI).

Jesus emphasized to St. Faustina that all our works of mercy are to flow from our love for Him, and are to become a consistent pattern in our lives. **You are to show mercy to your neighbors always and everywhere. You must not shrink from this or try to excuse yourself from it** (*Diary*, 742).

This would be an impossible command were it not that the more we humble ourselves and trust in The Divine Mercy, the more we receive the graces we need to let that mercy flow through us to others. Jesus assures us of this: **I am Love and Mercy itself. When a soul approaches Me with trust, I fill it with such an abundance of graces that it cannot contain them within itself, but radiates them to other souls** (*Diary*, 1074).

LIVING THE LORD'S PRAYER

Once, when Jesus was praying in a certain place (see Lk 11:1), the sight of what He was doing fascinated His disciples, "Lord, what do You say when You pray? Teach us to pray," one of the disciples blurted out. And so, Jesus taught them, but He did more than give them words to say; He gave them a way to live, the way He Himself lived — as Mercy Incarnate.

Jesus lived for His Father, pleasing Him, doing His will to reveal Him as a Father, rich in mercy (see Eph 2:4). In revealing God as Father, He was proclaiming and establishing the kingdom of God, and in this way, He hallowed the name of the Father and did His will. He trusted in the Father to provide all His needs each day, and He forgave all who hurt Him. By His redemption on the cross, He forgave us our sins (see Col 1:14), and by His daily living of trust and mercy, He destroyed the power of the Evil One. In a word, he lived and revealed *mercy*.

And so for us, too, the Lord's Prayer is a way to live. We can look at this prayer and see two pivotal points: the *Father* and the *kingdom*. Our whole life is to be for the Father. His kingdom is established as we follow Him and do His will. Prayer teaches us how to do His will — by totally trusting in Him for our daily bread; that is, all our daily needs, and by being merciful as He is merciful, forgiving others' sins as we are forgiven ours. This way, we are not put to the test, but are delivered from the prince of this world, the Evil One.

We are merciful by being continuously forgiving — 70 times seven a day! Forgiving in all the great and "little" things of our daily lives, forgiving ourselves, friends, family, co-workers, and even God for situations that displease us. Every time we feel ourselves getting impatient, angry, frustrated, we have an opportunity to forgive — an opportunity to cry, "I repent, I forgive." I repent for my part in this situation, and I forgive them for their part — Jesus, mercy!"

A beautiful example of being merciful by forgiving comes out in an incident between two women at a bookshop.

The owner came into the bookshop one day, and started direct-
ing the work of the manager, and this with her usual gusto. The
manager started to fume inside while trying to keep her cool on
the outside. Afterwards, she went to her parish priest and vented
her feelings about the interference in her work. After she had
vented her anger for a while, Father interrupted with the
question, "Was the owner right or wrong?"

"She was wrong!" retorted the woman with no uncer-
tainty in her voice.

"Wonderful," Father responded, "now you are in the
perfect situation to be a Christian and forgive her!"

To be merciful is to forgive without considering the right-
ness or the wrongness of the situation! This is the way Christ has
forgiven us, and the way we are to forgive one another.

PART II
The Devotion to
The Divine Mercy

In revealing, through St. Faustina, the special urgency of the message of mercy for our times, Our Lord also revealed special ways of living out our response to His mercy.

In addition to a renewed emphasis on the Sacraments of Eucharist and Reconciliation, these special means of drawing upon His mercy include the Image of The Divine Mercy, the Chaplet of The Divine Mercy, The Feast of Mercy, the Novena of Mercy, and prayer at the three o'clock hour — the hour of His death. All of these are elements of what we call the devotion to The Divine Mercy.

Devotion to The Divine Mercy is not "just another devotion;" rather, it is what a devotion ought to be according to the root meaning of the word — a consecration, a dedication by vow. Devotion to The Divine Mercy is a total commitment to God who is Mercy itself. It is a covenant of mercy, a continuously renewed promise to trust in the mercy of God and to be merciful just as He is merciful. In so doing, we receive the blessing of the beatitude which has been called a summary of the whole gospel, "Blessed are the merciful, for they shall obtain mercy" (Mt 5:7 RSV).

THE HOLY EUCHARIST,
THE PRESENCE OF MERCY

All the good that is in me is due to Holy Communion. I owe everything to it. I feel that this holy fire has transformed me completely. Oh, how happy I am to be a dwelling place for You, O Lord! My heart is a temple in which You dwell continually ... (*Diary*, 1392).

The Holy Eucharist is central to devotion to The Divine Mercy, so much so that Our Lord specifically asks, through St. Faustina, that we all receive Communion on the Feast of The Divine Mercy, after preparing for it through the Sacrament of Reconciliation. In the Eucharist, Jesus (Mercy Incarnate) is present Body and Blood, Soul and Divinity. The Eucharist is God's sacrificial gift of mercy, offered in atonement for our sins and those of the whole world; and in receiving it in Holy Communion, we are strengthened and consoled by the Lord who is Mercy itself.

Pope John Paul II spoke of these three aspects of the Eucharist — presence, sacrifice, and communion — as essential to our understanding of our faith (see *Redeemer of Man*). The presence of the Lord calls for our adoration, the sacrifice calls for our offering of ourselves with Christ, and Communion calls us to live in union with Him. Then, in his last encyclical, John Paul II calls the Eucharist "a mystery of mercy" (see *Ecclesia de Eucharistia*, chapter 2).

Through her life and writings, St. Faustina gives us a perfect model for responding to this threefold call of Jesus in the Eucharist; the Eucharist was so central to her life that she referred to it in some way on most of the pages of her *Diary* and wrote 16 beautiful prayers of preparation for Holy Communion (see *Diary*, 1804-1826).

ADORATION

Saint Faustina's adoration of the Eucharist began with the recognition of the great mystery of the Mass itself, and she urges us to special reverence and participation:

> Oh, what awesome mysteries take place during Mass! A great mystery is accomplished in the Holy Mass. With what great devotion should we listen to and take part in this death of Jesus. One day we will know what God is doing for us in each Mass, and what sort of gift He is preparing in it for us. Only His divine love could permit that such a gift be provided for us (*Diary*, 914).

During her working day, St. Faustina used every free moment to stop before the Blessed Sacrament and visit the Lord. She also spent special hours of adoration interceding for other people, especially those lost in sin.

These hours spent in adoration before the Blessed Sacrament resulted in a special Litany of Adoration of the Eucharist, which she wrote in 1935, emphasizing the Eucharist as the Mystery of Mercy (see *Diary*, 356).

OFFERING

One year, on Holy Thursday, St. Faustina saw, in a vision, the institution of the Eucharistic in the cenacle and was given to understand that in the offering that Jesus made of Himself on the night before He died, the sacrifice was fully consummated:

> I was most deeply moved when, before the Consecration, Jesus raised His eyes to heaven and entered into a mysterious conversation with His Father. It is only in eternity that we shall really understand that moment ... . At the moment of Consecration, love rested satiated — the sacrifice fully consummated. Now only the external ceremony

of death will be carried out — external destruction; the essence [of it] is in the Cenacle (*Diary*, 684).

This means then, that the Eucharistic *offering* is the essence of the sacrifice of Jesus. In every Mass, united with the priest, we offer the very Body and Blood, Soul and Divinity of our Lord Jesus Christ, made present on the altar by the words and actions of the priest through the power of The Holy Spirit. We unite the offering of ourselves with His offering, which is already accepted by the Father, and is made present to us here and now.

During Exposition of the Blessed Sacrament and during Mass itself, St. Faustina regularly saw our Lord. Most often she saw Him as a child; but at times, He appeared with rays of light as in the Image of The Divine Mercy; and at other times, she saw Him in His Passion and was able to participate in it with Him, sharing His pain:

Today, from early morning, divine absorption penetrates my soul. During Mass, I thought I would see the little Jesus, as I often do; however, today during Holy Mass I saw the Crucified Jesus. Jesus was nailed to the cross and was in great agony. His suffering pierced me, soul and body, in a manner which was invisible, but nevertheless most painful (*Diary*, 913, February 2, 1937).

UNION

Uniting herself to Jesus through the regular reception of Communion, St. Faustina learned to draw all her strength and consolation from the Eucharist, a lesson that is important for us to learn as well:

One thing alone sustains me, and that is Holy Communion. From it I draw my strength; in it is all my comfort … . Jesus concealed in the Host is everything to me. From the tabernacle I draw strength, power, courage and light. Here, I seek consolation in time of anguish. I would not know how to give glory

to God if I did not have the Eucharist in my heart
(*Diary*, 1037).

As the battle of each day began, she found renewed
confidence and strength in the Eucharist:

> Every morning during meditation, I prepare myself
> for the whole day's struggle. Holy Communion
> assures me that I will win the victory; and so it is. ...
> This Bread of the Strong gives me all the strength I
> need to carry on my mission and the courage to do
> whatever the Lord asks of me. The courage and
> strength that are in me are not of me, but of Him
> who lives in me — it is the Eucharist (*Diary*, 91).

She learned, too, that the Lord continued to live in her
— continued to be present in her, as in a tabernacle, until her
next reception of the Holy Eucharist in Holy Communion:

> Today, I have come to understand many of God's
> mysteries. I have come to know that Holy
> Communion remains in me until the next Holy
> Communion. A vivid and clearly felt presence of God
> continues in my soul. The awareness of this plunges
> me into deep recollection, without the slightest
> effort on my part. My heart is a living tabernacle in
> which the living Host is reserved. I have never
> sought God in some far-off place, but within myself.
> It is in the depths of my own being that I commune
> with my God (*Diary*, 1302, September 29, 1937).

On more than one occasion, the Lord shared with her
how closely He wants to unite Himself with us through the
Eucharist, if only we would recognize His presence:

> **My great delight is to unite Myself with souls ...
> when I come to a human heart in Holy
> Communion, My hands are full of all kinds of
> graces which I want to give to the soul. But souls**

do not even pay any attention to Me; they leave Me to Myself and busy themselves with other things. Oh, how sad I am that souls do not recognize Love! They treat Me as a dead object (*Diary*, 1385).

Saint Faustina's recognition of the reality of Christ's presence in the Eucharist and her unconditional "yes" to His call for sacrifice and unity should be an inspiration to us all to re-examine our own response to His great Sacrament, in which the Lord of mercy pours Himself into our hearts:

I often feel God's presence after Holy Communion in a special and tangible way. I know God is in my heart. And the fact that I feel Him in my heart does not interfere with my duties. Even when I am dealing with very important matters which require attention, I do not lose the presence of God in my soul, and I am closely united with Him. With Him, I go to work, with Him I go for recreation, with Him I suffer, with Him I rejoice; I live in Him and He in me. I am never alone, because He is my constant companion. He is present to me at every moment (*Diary*, 318).

RECONCILIATION: THE TRIBUNAL OF MERCY

Since we are weak human beings and we do sin ("even the just man falls seven times a day"), the Lord has provided a Sacrament of Mercy through which He forgives us and heals us when we fall and are wounded. He spoke repeatedly to St. Faustina about using the Sacrament of Reconciliation as a "Tribunal of Mercy," wherein we receive a judgment, not of condemnation, but of love and mercy:

Tell souls where they are to look for solace; that is, in the Tribunal of Mercy [the Sacrament of Reconciliation]. **There the greatest miracles take place** [and] **are incessantly repeated** (*Diary*, 1448).

The term "Tribunal of Mercy" comes from the tradition of the Roman court of three judges. In the Sacrament of Reconciliation, the priest represents the three Persons of the Holy Trinity: the Father, Son, and Holy Spirit. God Himself brings us mercy.

Our Lord made it clear to her that we don't have to make great pilgrimages or involve ourselves in other external ceremonies in order to receive these miracles of His mercy and forgiveness:

It suffices to come with faith to the feet of My representative and to reveal to him one's misery, and the miracle of Divine Mercy will be fully demonstrated (*Diary*, 1448).

The Sacrament of Reconciliation became a regular and important part of her life, and she grew in her understanding of it. She learned that Confession is much more than just asking and receiving forgiveness. "We should desire two kinds of profit from Holy Confession." she explained:

1. We come to Confession to be healed;
2. We come to be educated — like a small child, our soul has constant need of education (*Diary*, 377).

She realized that this need of our souls for education — through the grace of God and through the guidance of the confessor — is vital to our spiritual growth. We cannot simply rely on ourselves:

On its own strength, the soul will not go far; it will exert itself greatly and will do nothing for the glory of God; it will err continually, because our mind is darkened and does not know how to discern its own affairs (*Diary*, 377).

Another important lesson St.Faustina learned was to pray for her confessor:

> I came to understand one thing: that I must pray much for each of my confessors, that he might obtain the light of the Holy Spirit, for when I approach the confessional without first praying fervently, the confessor does not understand me very well. Father encouraged me to pray fervently for these intentions, that God would give better knowledge and understanding of the things He is asking of me (*Diary*, 647).

Through St. Faustina, Christ Himself instructs us how to prepare for the reception of the Sacrament:

> **When you go to confession, to this fountain of My mercy, the Blood and Water which came forth from My Heart always flows down upon your soul and ennobles it. Every time you go to confession, immerse yourself entirely in My mercy, with great trust, so that I may pour the bounty of My grace upon your soul** (*Diary*, 1602).

Repeatedly, He emphasized that the confessional is the place of the greatest mercy, and that it is He, Himself, Mercy Incarnate, who waits for us there:

> **When you approach the confessional, know this, that I Myself am waiting there for you. I am only hidden by the priest, but I Myself act in your soul. Here the misery of the soul meets the God of mercy** (*Diary*, 1602).

> **My daughter, just as you prepare in My presence, so also you make your confession before Me. The person of the priest is, for Me, only a screen. Never analyze what sort of a priest it is that I am making use of; open your soul in confession as you would to Me, and I will fill it with My light** (*Diary*, 1725).

He stresses, too, that no matter how great our sin, His mercy is greater and can restore us to His grace:

> **Were a soul like a decaying corpse so that from a human standpoint, there would be no [hope of] restoration and everything would already be lost, it is not so with God. The miracle of Divine Mercy restores that soul in full** (*Diary*, 1448).

Our sinfulness, then, cannot keep us from receiving His mercy. Only our fear and refusal to trust in Him can block His love. So our Lord urges St. Faustina:

> **Pray for souls that they be not afraid to approach the tribunal of My Mercy. Do not grow weary of praying for sinners** (*Diary*, 975).

> **Tell souls that from this fount of mercy souls draw graces solely with the vessel of trust. If their trust is great, there is no limit to My generosity** (*Diary*, 1602).

The Church, likewise, continues to exhort us to make frequent use of this Sacrament of Reconciliation, even monthly, to draw on this infinite fount of mercy. John Paul II had a special concern that we make use of the Sacrament and be healed of one of the great sins of our age — the loss of the sense of sin.

Our Lord emphasized the importance of the Sacrament by making its reception one of the conditions for celebrating the Feast of mercy:

> **On that day, the very depths of My tender mercy are open. I pour out a whole ocean of graces upon those souls who approach the Fount of My Mercy. The soul that will go to Confession and receive Holy Communion shall obtain complete forgiveness of sins and punishment** (*Diary*, 699).

The Sacrament of Reconciliation in which we confess our sins is truly a place of receiving God's mercy — it really is a "Tribunal of Mercy."

THE IMAGE OF THE
DIVINE MERCY

I am offering people a vessel with which they are to keep coming for graces to the fountain of mercy. That vessel is this image with the signature: "Jesus, I trust in You" (*Diary,* 327).

After appearing to her in a vision, our Lord asked St. Faustina to have an image painted according to the pattern she saw; and He explained to her that this image would be a vessel to draw mercy from the infinite ocean of His mercy. The image is of Jesus coming toward us with His right hand raised in blessing and His left hand touching His garment in the area of the heart where two great rays of light shine forth, one red and the other pale. He is dressed in a white garment and is radiant with light. (Copies of the restored image of The Divine Mercy painted under the direction of St. Faustina are now available).

This image is an icon of Jesus as eternal High Priest, dressed in the white robes of the priest, coming with His hands raised in blessing, coming with salvation for those who await Him, coming with the gifts of life-giving water, blood, and the Spirit. The icon presents three scenes from Scripture, simultaneously, like a triple-exposed photograph.

The most obvious scene is that of Easter Sunday night when Jesus appeared in the upper room, coming through the locked doors of the cenacle, coming with the victorious blessings of peace, showing His wounds, giving to His apostles the authority that He had received, breathing on them the Holy Spirit for the forgiveness of sins (see Jn 20:19-31).

The second scene is Jesus at Calvary with His side pierced, blood and water flowing out as a fount of mercy for us — here seen as the red and pale rays representing the waters of Baptism and the Blood of the Eucharist (see Jn 19:31-37).

The third scene is Jesus as the Eternal High Priest, dressed in the white linen of the priest coming out of the Holy of Holies — this time not from the sanctuary made by human hands, but from the Holy of Holies of Heaven, the very Mercy Seat of the Father. He comes as the "Merciful One" with blessing in His raised hand and the name of the Lord on His lips (see Sir 50:18-21 and Lv 16:1-4).

Jesus our High Priest "was offered once to take away the sins of [the] many: He will appear a second time to bring salvation to those who eagerly await Him" (Heb 9:28 RSV). He will come to bring the culmination of *mercy to those who await Him.*

When He asked St. Faustina to have the image painted, our Lord insisted that a special inscription be included at the bottom of the painting, and He made several promises for those who would venerate His mercy through this image:

> **Paint an image according to the pattern you see, with the signature: Jesus, I trust in You! I desire that this image be venerated, first in your chapel, and [then] throughout the world. I promise that the soul that will venerate this image will not perish. I also promise victory over [its] enemies already here on earth, especially at the hour of death. I, Myself, will defend it as My own glory** (*Diary,* 47-48, February 22, 1931).

The word signature suggests that the image should be signed just as you would sign a contract. So a beautiful way for us to venerate the image of The Divine Mercy is to actually sign the image with the inscription, *Jesus, I trust in You!* along with our own name and date. This signing of our pledge of trust in Jesus is our part of the solemn contract, called the

New Covenant or New Testament. Jesus, on His part, has already completed the covenant by sealing His gift of mercy with His blood. Our first and foremost response to His mercy is to trust in Him. His mercy is infinite; our trust must also be boundless and complete.

The Holy Spirit is always available to help us in our weakness if we ask Him with faith and so, we ask, "Come, Holy Spirit, fill us with trust in the Merciful Jesus"

The signed image of The Divine Mercy hung in our homes or kept in our prayer books can be a daily reminder that we have solemnly promised, "Jesus, I trust in You" — always and everywhere.

Some people have expressed a preference of one image over another, asking why it cannot be like the original. Such sentiments are not new. The original image, now hanging in a church in Lithuania, was such a disappointment to St. Faustina that she even complained to the Lord about it. Many artists have since tried to follow her directions in giving their interpretation of the Merciful Savior. To them and to all of us, our Lord's answer to St. Faustina serves as a strong reminder not to let any one painting of The Divine Mercy become more important than the reality it represents:

> Once, when I was visiting the artist [Eugene Kazimirowski] who was painting the image, and saw that it was not as beautiful as Jesus is, I felt very sad about it, but I hid this deep in my heart. When we had left the artist's house, Mother Superior [Irene] stayed in town to attend to some matters while I returned home alone. I went immediately to the chapel and wept a good deal. I said to the Lord, "Who will paint You as beautiful as You are?" Then I heard these words: **"Not in the beauty of the color, nor of the brush lies the greatness of this image, but in My grace"** (*Diary*, 313).

THE CHAPLET OF THE DIVINE MERCY

+ The Lord's Promise: **The souls that will say this chaplet will be embraced by My mercy during their lifetime and especially at the hour of their death** (*Diary*, 754).

The Chaplet of The Divine Mercy is an intercessory prayer that extends the offering of the Eucharist, and so it is a priestly prayer, prayed on the rosary beads beginning with the Our Father, Hail Mary, and the Creed. Then on the large beads we pray:

> **Eternal Father, I offer You the Body and Blood, Soul and Divinity of Your Dearly Beloved Son, Our Lord, Jesus Christ, in atonement for our sins and those of the whole world.**

On the small beads we pray:

> **For the sake of His sorrowful Passion, have mercy on us and on the whole world.**

And at the end, we pray three times:

> **Holy God, Holy Mighty One, Holy Immortal One, have mercy on us and on the whole world** (*Diary*, 476).

The words of the chaplet reflect the Council of Trent's dogmatic definition of the Real Presence in the Eucharist and the text of 1 John 2:2: "He is the atoning sacrifice for our sins, and not only ours, but also for the sins of the whole world." And the doxology concluding the chaplet is one of the most ancient intercessory prayers addressed to the Most

Holy Trinity — used most widely in the churches of the Byzantine Rite, and Good Friday in the Roman Rite.

The chaplet can be recited or chanted using various melodies. A traditional melody has been used by the Sisters of Our Lady of Mercy in Krakow for many years.

ORIGIN OF THE CHAPLET

In 1935, St. Faustina received the words of the chaplet in a vision. She saw an angel of God on a mission to execute the wrath of God. She was taken up before the throne of God and began to plead with Him for mercy for the world, praying with words she heard interiorly:

> As I was praying in this manner, I saw the Angel's help-lessness: he could not carry out the just punishment which was rightly due for sins. Never before had I prayed with such inner power as I did then. The words with which I entreated God are these: **Eternal Father, I offer You the Body and Blood, Soul and Divinity of Your dearly beloved Son, Our Lord Jesus Christ, in atonement for our sins and those of the whole world; for the sake of His sorrowful Passion, have mercy on us** (*Diary*, 474-475).

Our Lord asked St. Faustina to encourage us to pray the chaplet, and He renewed His Gospel promise to answer our prayer:

> **My daughter, encourage souls to say the chaplet which I have given to you. It pleases Me to grant everything they ask of Me by saying the chaplet** (*Diary*, 1541).

Our Lord then went on to make His promise specific for those trapped in sin:

> **When hardened sinners say it, I will fill their souls with peace, and the hour of their death will be a**

happy one. **Write this for the benefit of distressed souls: when a soul sees and realizes the gravity of its sins, when the whole abyss of the misery into which it immersed itself is displayed before its eyes, let it not despair, but with trust let it throw itself into the arms of My mercy, as a child into the arms of its beloved mother. These souls have a right of priority to My compassionate Heart, they have priority to My mercy. Tell them that no soul that has called upon My mercy has been disappointed or brought to shame. I delight particularly in a soul which has placed its trust in My goodness** (*Diary*, 1541).

He then turns to the need of those attending to the dying:

Write that when they say this chaplet in the presence of the dying, I will stand between My Father and the dying person, not as the just Judge but as the merciful Savior (*Diary*, 1541).

On a number of occasions, our Lord asked St. Faustina to pray for the dying by praying the chaplet until the person was in peace. She was repeatedly told to recommend the chaplet especially to priests in their ministry to the dying:

Once, as I was going down the hall to the kitchen, I heard these words in my soul: **Say unceasingly the chaplet that I have taught you. Whoever will recite it will receive great mercy at the hour of death. Priests will recommend it to sinners as their last hope of salvation. Even if there were a sinner most hardened, if he recites this chaplet only once, he will receive grace from My infinite mercy. I desire that the whole world know My infinite mercy. I desire to grant unimaginable graces to those souls who trust in My mercy** (*Diary*, 687).

Saint Faustina prayed the chaplet for the needs of nature — for rain, for protection against storms:

> When a great storm was approaching, I began to say the chaplet. Suddenly I heard the voice of an angel: "I cannot approach in this storm, because the light which comes from her mouth drives back both me and the storm." Such was the angel's complaint to God. I then recognized how much havoc he was to have made through this storm; but I also recognized that *this prayer was pleasing to God, and that this chaplet was most powerful* (*Diary*, 1791, emphasis added).

It really is a powerful prayer, and our Lord gave this prayer to St. Faustina so that we could use it. We can all use the chaplet to cry out for mercy on the world, crying out in union with Mass as we offer the Body and Blood, Soul and Divinity of our Lord Jesus Christ in atonement for our sins and those of the whole world.

THE FEAST OF THE DIVINE MERCY

I desire that the first Sunday after Easter be the Feast of Mercy (*Diary*, 299).

+Ask of my faithful servant [Father Sopocko] that, on this day, he tell the whole world of My great mercy; that whoever approaches the Fount of Life on this day will be granted complete remission of sins and punishment.

+Mankind will not have peace until it turns with trust to My mercy (*Diary*, 300).

Our Lord asked St. Faustina to pray and to work to have
established a Feast of The Divine Mercy on the Sunday after
Easter. This would be a day of total forgiveness of sins for
those who approach the Eucharist and the Sacrament of
Reconciliation. It would be an annual celebration like the Day
of Atonement. All sins and punishment would be washed
away in His infinite mercy. Interestingly enough, the texts of
the liturgy for that Sunday already focus on the forgiveness of
sins. (The Gospel is of Jesus appearing in the upper room and
bestowing the authority to forgive sins; and the other readings
also refer to mercy, Ps 118, and 1 Pt 1:3-9.)

Our Lord spoke to St. Faustina about the special purpose
of the feast as a "refuge and shelter for all souls" and described
how His mercy was especially available to all who call upon it
on that day:

> **My daughter, tell the whole world about My
> inconceivable mercy. I desire that the Feast of
> Mercy be a refuge and shelter for all souls, and
> especially for poor sinners. On that day the very
> depths of My tender mercy are open. I pour out a
> whole ocean of graces upon those souls who
> approach the fount of My Mercy. The soul that will
> go to Confession** [sometime during the Lenten
> Season] **and receive Holy Communion shall obtain
> complete forgiveness of sins and punishment. On
> that day are open all the divine floodgates through
> which graces flow. Let no soul fear to draw near to
> Me, even though its sins be as scarlet. My mercy is
> so great that no mind, be it of man or of angel, will
> be able to fathom it throughout eternity.
> Everything that exists has come forth from the very
> depths of My most tender mercy. Every soul in its
> relation to Me will contemplate My love and mercy
> throughout eternity. The Feast of Mercy emerged
> from My very depths of tenderness. It is My desire
> that it be solemnly celebrated on the first Sunday**

after Easter. Mankind will not have peace until it turns to the Fount of My Mercy (*Diary*, 699).

Again, our Lord spoke of the conditions for receiving His special mercy on the Feast:

I want to grant a complete pardon to the souls that will go to Confession and receive Holy Communion on the Feast of My mercy (*Diary*, 1109).

Jesus made it clear to St. Faustina that He was very serious about this Feast of Mercy — His desire and plan is to have mercy on all:

This morning during Holy Mass, I saw the Suffering Jesus. His Passion was imprinted on my body in an invisible manner, but no less painfully. Jesus looked at me and said, **Souls perish in spite of My bitter Passion. I am giving them the last hope of salvation; that is, the Feast of My Mercy. If they will not adore My mercy, write, tell souls about this great mercy of Mine, because the awful day, the day of My justice, is near** (*Diary*, 964-965).

Say, My daughter, that the Feast of My Mercy has issued forth from My very depths for the consolation of the whole world (*Diary*, 1517).

All of us can celebrate the Sunday after Easter as a day of mercy, responding to the desire of our Lord and the exhortation of Pope John Paul II, who in his encyclical *Rich in Mercy*, declared:

... At no time and in no historical period — especially at a moment as critical as our own — can the Church forget the prayer that is a cry for the mercy of God amid the many forms of evil which weigh upon humanity and threaten it. ... Loud cries should be the mark of the Church of our times, *cries uttered to God to implore His Mercy* ... (VIII, 15).

In fact, on Sunday, April 30, 2000, at the canonization of St. Faustina, John Paul II also "canonized" The Divine Mercy message and devotion by declaring the Second Sunday of Easter as "Divine Mercy Sunday" for the universal Church. Of Divine Mercy Sunday, he said in his homily: "It is important that we accept the whole message that comes to us from the Word of God on this Second Sunday of Easter, which from now on throughout the Church will be called 'Divine Mercy Sunday.'"

More than 15,000 people attend the annual Divine Mercy Sunday Weekend at the National Shrine of The Divine Mercy on the grounds of the Marian Fathers of the Immaculate Conception in Stockbridge, Massachusetts.

The Shrine's celebration of Divine Mercy Sunday is the largest such observance in the Northeast and one of the largest in the world. The Holy Mass is broadcast around the world on EWTN, the Catholic global cable network.

THE NOVENA TO THE DIVINE MERCY

In preparation for the Feast of The Divine Mercy, the Lord asked St. Faustina to make a novena of prayer from Good Friday to the following Saturday:

> **I desire that during these nine days you bring souls to the fountain of My mercy, that they may draw therefrom strength and refreshment and whatever grace they need in the hardships of life and, especially, at the hour of death.**

> **On each day, you will bring to My Heart a different group of souls, and you will immerse them in this ocean of My mercy, and I will bring all these souls into the house of My Father. You will do this in this life and in the next. I will deny**

nothing to any soul whom you will bring to the fount of My mercy. On each day, you will beg My Father, on the strength of My bitter Passion, for graces for these souls (*Diary*, 1209).

When St. Faustina answered that she did not know how to make this novena, Jesus replied that He would tell her which souls to bring each day into His Heart. It is important to note that the laity can lead the novena and free the priest for his ministerial duties:

FIRST DAY

Today bring to Me all mankind, especially all sinners, and immerse them in the ocean of My mercy. In this way you will console Me in the bitter grief into which the loss of souls plunges Me (*Diary*, 1210).

SECOND DAY

Today bring to Me the souls of priests and religious, and immerse them in My unfathomable mercy. It was they who gave Me strength to endure My bitter Passion. Through them as through channels My mercy flows out upon mankind (*Diary*, 1212).

THIRD DAY

Today bring to Me all devout and faithful souls, and immerse them in the ocean of My mercy. These souls brought Me consolation on the Way of the Cross. They were that drop of consolation in the midst of an ocean of bitterness (*Diary*, 1214).

FOURTH DAY

Today bring to Me those who do not believe in Me and those who do not yet know Me. I was thinking also of them during My bitter Passion, and their future zeal comforted My Heart. Immerse them in the ocean of My mercy (*Diary*, 1216).

FIFTH DAY

Today bring to Me the souls of those who have separated themselves from My Church, and immerse them in the ocean of My mercy. During My bitter Passion they tore at My Body and Heart; that is, My Church. As they return to unity with the Church, My wounds heal, and in this way they alleviate My Passion (*Diary*, 1218).

SIXTH DAY

Today bring to Me the meek and humble souls and the souls of little children, and immerse them in My mercy. These souls most closely resemble My Heart. They strengthened Me during My bitter agony. I saw them as earthly Angels, who would keep vigil at My altars. I pour out upon them whole torrents of grace. Only the humble soul is capable of receiving My grace. I favor humble souls with My confidence (*Diary*, 1220).

SEVENTH DAY

Today bring to Me the souls who especially venerate and glorify My mercy, and immerse them in My mercy. These souls sorrowed most over My Passion and entered most deeply into My Spirit. They are living images of My Compassionate Heart. These souls will shine with a special brightness in the next life. Not one of them will go into the fire of hell. I shall particularly defend each one of them at the hour of death (*Diary*, 1224).

EIGHTH DAY

Today bring to Me the souls who are in the prison of Purgatory, and immerse them in the abyss of My mercy. Let the torrents of My Blood cool down their scorching flames. All these souls are greatly loved by Me. They are making retribution to My justice. It is in your power to bring them relief. Draw all the indulgences from the treasury of My Church and offer them on their behalf. Oh, if you only knew the torments they suffer, you would continually offer for them the alms of the spirit and pay off their debt to My justice (*Diary*, 1226).

NINTH DAY

Today bring to Me souls who have become lukewarm, and immerse them in the abyss of My mercy. These souls wound My Heart most painfully. My soul suffered the most dreadful loathing in the Garden of Olives because of lukewarm souls. They were the reason I cried out: "Father, take this cup away from Me, if it be Your will." For them the last hope of salvation is to flee to My mercy (*Diary*, 1228).

The novena prayers, written by St. Faustina, have been popular among many, but it is important to realize that they are not the central element of the devotion. Our Lord asked St. Faustina to make a novena for the intentions He gave her, making to her sweeping promises. For us, the request is more for a novena of chaplets. Our Lord told St. Faustina:

By this novena [of chaplets] I will grant every possible grace to souls (*Diary*, 796).

Certainly, this does not mean that we shouldn't use St. Faustina's novena prayers. At the National Shrine of The Divine Mercy in Stockbridge, Massachusetts, as in Poland and many other places around the world, the novena from Good Friday to Mercy Sunday is an annual solemn celebration. Further, at the National Shrine in Stockbridge, the Marian Fathers pray a perpetual novena of chaplets to The Divine Mercy. So the daily intentions for her novena can also be used for prayer at any time, especially with the chaplet.

You can make a continuous novena of chaplets. Beginning on a Friday with the intentions given by our Lord to St. Faustina, you would continue until the following Saturday. That gives you five days for your own special intentions before you begin once again on the next Friday with the intentions given by our Lord. Here are some examples:

- Sunday for *Peace* in the hearts of people and in the world.

- Monday for *the Holy Father*, that his words be heard and that he be given greater courage and faith.

- Tuesday for *Bishops*, that they be united in heart and mind

- Wednesday for communities of religious and laity, that they be zealous for the Lord and united.

- Thursday for *families*, that they be protected from the attack of secularism.

Each of us can thus use the intentions for each day as our Lord directs us and so intercede for the whole Church and world.

THE THREE O'CLOCK PRAYER FOR MERCY

At three o'clock, implore My mercy, especially for sinners; and, if only for a brief moment, immerse yourself in My Passion, particularly in My abandonment at the moment of agony. This is the hour of great mercy for the whole world. I will allow you to enter into My mortal sorrow. In this hour, I will refuse nothing to the soul that makes a request of Me in virtue of My Passion ... (*Diary*, 1320).

The Lord asked St. Faustina to pray especially for sinners at three o'clock in the afternoon, the moment of His death on the cross. This is the hour of great mercy for the world, and can be a moment of reflection on His Passion and death for us. If possible, it is a good time to make a visit to the Blessed Sacrament and an excellent time for making the Stations of the Cross:

> **I remind you, My daughter, that as often as you hear the clock strike the third hour, immerse yourself completely in My mercy, adoring and glorifying it; invoke its omnipotence for the whole world, and particularly for poor sinners; for at that moment mercy was opened wide for every soul. In this hour, you can obtain everything for yourself and for others for the asking; it was the hour of grace for the whole world — mercy triumphed over justice.**

> **My daughter, try your best to make the Stations of the Cross in this hour, provided that your duties permit it; and if you are not able to make the Stations of the Cross, then at least step into the chapel for a moment and adore, in the Blessed Sacrament, My Heart, which is full of mercy; and should you be unable to step into the chapel, immerse yourself in prayer there where you happen to be, if only for a very brief instant. I claim veneration of My mercy from every creature ... (*Diary*, 1572).**

THREE O'CLOCK PRAYER FOR MERCY AT THE NATIONAL SHRINE OF THE DIVINE MERCY

Each day at the National Shrine in Stockbridge, you can hear the bells at three o'clock, calling people to prayer — a brief moment of prayer while working or, for those who can, a pause from work to participate in the special three o'clock prayers at the Shrine.

As the sound of the bells fades away, the leader begins with the sign of the cross, and together we pray:

> You expired, Jesus, but the source of life gushed forth for souls, and the ocean of mercy opened up for the whole world. O Fount of Life, unfathomable Divine Mercy, envelop the whole world and empty Yourself out upon us (*Diary*, 1319).

And then, three times,

> O Blood and Water, which gushed forth from the Heart of Jesus, as a fount of mercy for us, I trust in You (*Diary*, 84).

Then follows the recitation of the chaplet with the leader praying the first half of the Our Father and Hail Mary and all responding with the second half; then all together reciting the Creed. In turn, five from those present will each lead a decade:

Leader:

> Eternal Father,
> I offer you the Body and Blood,
> Soul and Divinity
> of Your dearly beloved Son,
> Our Lord Jesus Christ,

All:

> in atonement for our sins
> and those of the whole world.

Then we pray 10 times:

Leader:

> For the sake of His sorrowful Passion

All:

> have mercy on us and on the whole world.

At the conclusion of five such decades, we pray together:

All:

> Holy God, Holy Mighty One, Holy Immortal One,
> have mercy on us and on the whole world. (3 times)

After the chaplet, two concluding prayers, drawn from
St. Faustina's Diary are recited:

LET US PRAY

All:

> Eternal God, in whom mercy is endless and the
> treasury of compassion inexhaustible, look kindly upon
> us and increase Your mercy in us, that in difficult
> moments we might not despair nor become despon-
> dent, but with great confidence submit ourselves to
> Your holy will, which is Love and Mercy itself. Amen
> (*Diary*, 950).

A PRAYER FOR DIVINE MERCY

All:

> O Greatly Merciful God, Infinite Goodness, today all
> mankind calls out from the abyss of its misery to
> Your mercy — to Your compassion, O God; and it is
> with its mighty voice of misery that it cries out.
> Gracious God, do not reject the prayer of this earth's
> exiles! O Lord, Goodness beyond our understand-
> ing, Who are acquainted with out misery through
> and through, and know that by our own power we
> cannot ascend to You, we implore You: anticipate us
> with Your grace and keep on increasing Your mercy
> in us, that we may faithfully do Your holy will all
> through our life and at death's hour. Let the
> omnipotence of Your mercy shield us from the darts
> of our salvation's enemies, that we may with confi-

dence, as Your children, await Your final coming —
that day known to You alone. And we expect to
obtain everything promised us by Jesus in spite of all
our wretchedness. For Jesus is our Hope: Through
His merciful Heart, as through an open gate, we pass
through to heaven (*Diary*, 1570).

All of us can take advantage of the tremendous promises
of grace at the three o'clock hour, crying out for mercy on the
whole world.

PART III
Apostles of Mercy

The message of mercy says we are to be merciful — even as the Father is merciful. This is the essence of being an apostle of mercy. In Part I, we saw how we are to be merciful to others. Then, in Part II, we saw various ways by which we can practice and grow in God's mercy. In Part III, we consider the special place of suffering, intercession, and the proclamation of mercy in the life of St. Faustina whom our Lord called to be the Apostle of Mercy. We will also see how Our Blessed Mother taught St. Faustina to fulfill that role.

REDEMPTIVE SUFFERING

I have been crucified with Christ; it is no longer I who live, but Christ who lives in me; and the life I live now in the flesh, I live by faith in the Son or God, who loved me and gave Himself for me (Gal 2:20 RSV).

Suffering is a most unpopular subject, because so many of us don't understand the meaning of suffering. We don't like it, we don't want it, and we don't even want to talk about it. Yet it is at the heart of our redemption. Like it or not, our salvation took place on the cross.

The mercy given us didn't come easy. It was made available to us by the redemptive suffering of Jesus Christ, together with the sufferings of St. Faustina and many others like her, who unite their sufferings with Jesus for the sake of others.

Suffering has a meaning and a purpose. Christ invites us to share the cross: "If any man would come after Me, let him deny himself and take up his cross daily and follow Me" (Lk 9:23 RSV). We are told that it is our "special privilege to take Christ's part — not only to believe in Him, but also to suffer for Him" (Phil 1:29 NAB). Saint Paul even rejoices that by suffering he can make up what is lacking in the sufferings of Christ: "Even now, I find my joy in the sufferings I endure for you, in my own flesh I fill up what is lacking in the sufferings of Christ for the sake of His body, the Church" (Col 1:24, NAB). St. Paul could find joy in his sufferings because he knew that they had meaning.

And so, what is the meaning of suffering for a Christian? Pope John Paul II, in his Apostolic Letter *The Christian Meaning of Human Suffering*, 1984, wrote that Christ sanctified suffering, making it salvific by His love. Now the Lord invites us to be partners in the work of salvation by bringing His mercy to everyone. How? By offering our sufferings, no matter what kind or from what source, with love, uniting them with Christ for the salvation of others.

The saving work of Jesus is not finished. He "needs" us to cooperate with His work of redemption and bring His mercy to this generation. This kind of partnership involves a sharing in His sufferings in order to share in the saving work of mercy. This is the meaning of suffering. It is salvific; it is precious. Don't waste it!

Some people are specially chosen to become victim souls; that is, souls that willingly and freely ask to share in the sufferings of Christ for the sake of others. This is a very special vocation; not all of us are called in this way. But we *are* called to join our sufferings to the sufferings of Christ for the salvation of souls, applying the sufferings of Christ to the present situation. And even if our sufferings may differ in type and degree from what St. Faustina and other special souls are called to endure, we can profit from her example.

Saint Faustina understood very well that she was being invited to a life of sacrifice. It was an invitation to her that called for her free consent to the will of God, for the Lord always respects the freedom of an individual:

> A vision passed before the eyes of my soul; it was like the vision Jesus had in the Garden of Olives. First, the physical sufferings and all the circumstances that would increase them; [then] the full scope of the spiritual sufferings and those that no one would know about. Everything entered into the vision: false suspicions, loss of good name ... . My name is to be: "sacrifice."

> When the vision ended, a cold sweat bathed my forehead. Jesus made it known to me that even if I did not give my consent to this, I could still be saved; and He would not lessen His graces. ...

> The whole mystery depended on me, on my free consent to the sacrifice given with full use of my

faculties. In this free and conscious act lies the whole power and value before His Majesty. Even if none of these things for which I offered myself would ever happen to me, before the Lord everything was as though it had already been consummated.

At that moment, I realized I was entering into communion with the incomprehensible Majesty. I felt that God was waiting for my word, for my consent. Then my spirit immersed itself in the Lord, and I said, "Do with me as You please. I subject myself to Your will ..." (*Diary*, 135-136).

Saint Faustina was very well aware of how precious suffering was for saving souls. She willingly, and even eagerly, offered herself as a victim for the salvation of others. Through this total offering of herself, she became a powerful intercessor and apostle of mercy, especially for those who have lost hope in God's mercy, for she was able to share in the saving work of Christ.

Saint Faustina suffered terribly, not only from tuberculosis, but also from the remarks of her fellow sisters:

When I fell sick after my first vows and when, despite the kind and solicitous care of my Superiors and the efforts of the doctor, I felt neither better nor worse, remarks began to reach my ears which inferred that I was making believe. With that, my suffering was doubled, and this lasted for quite a long time. One day, I complained to Jesus that I was being a burden to the sisters. Jesus answered me, **You are not living for yourself but for souls, and other souls will profit from your sufferings. Your prolonged suffering will give them the light and strength to accept My will** (*Diary*, 67).

She offered all her sufferings with a burning longing for the salvation of souls:

O Jesus, I long for the salvation of immortal souls. It
is in sacrifice that my heart will find free expression,
in sacrifice which no one will suspect. I will burn and
be consumed unseen in the holy flames of the love of
God. The presence of God will help me sacrifice to
be perfect and pure (*Diary*, 235).

Her sufferings were not offered in an isolated way, but were
united with Christ crucified:

+ During Holy Mass, I saw the Lord Jesus nailed
upon the cross amidst great torments. A soft moan
issued from His Heart. After some time, He said, **I
thirst, I desire the salvation of souls. Help Me, My
daughter, to save souls. Join your sufferings to My
Passion and offer them to the heavenly Father for
sinners** (*Diary*, 1032).

For the sake of sinners, St.Faustina suffered the pain of the
wounds of Jesus, Himself.

For quite a long while, I felt pain in my hands, feet
and side. Then I saw a certain sinner who, profiting
from my sufferings, drew near to the Lord. All this
for starving souls that they may not die of starvation
(*Diary*, 1468).

When she offered a day for priests, it was the worst experience of suffering she ever had!

I have offered this day for priests. I have suffered more
than ever before, both interiorly and exteriorly. I did
not know it was possible to suffer so much in one
day. I tried to make a Holy Hour, in the course of
which my spirit had a taste of the bitterness of the
Garden of Gethsemane. I am fighting alone, sup-
ported by His arm, against all the difficulties that
face me like unassailable walls. But I trust in the
power of His name, and I fear nothing (*Diary*, 823).

Throughout her *Diary*, St. Faustina writes of her dealing with suffering, and it becomes clear that redemptive suffering for the salvation of souls was part of her mission. She learned that suffering was God's gift to her:

> Suffering is a great grace; through suffering the soul becomes like the Savior; in suffering, love becomes crystallized; the greater the suffering, the purer the love (*Diary*, 57).

She learned to accept both joy and suffering equally:

> I accept joy or suffering, praise or humiliation with the same disposition. I remember that one and the other are passing. What does it matter to me what people say about me? I have long ago given up everything that concerns my person. My name is host — or sacrifice, not in words but in deeds, in the emptying of myself and in becoming like You on the Cross, O good Jesus, my Master (*Diary*, 485).

She also learned how greatly God loves suffering souls:

> +Oh, if only the suffering soul knew how it is loved by God, it would die of joy and excess of happiness! Some day, we will know the value of suffering, but then we will no longer be able to suffer. The present moment is ours (*Diary*, 963).

Finally, as her death was approaching, St. Faustina offered herself as a holocaust for the spreading of the message of Divine Mercy:

> Today, I again offered myself to The Lord as a holocaust for sinners. My Jesus, if the end of my life is already approaching, I beg You most humbly, accept my death in union with You as a holocaust which I offer You today, while I still have full possession of my faculties and a fully conscious will, and this for a threefold purpose:

Firstly: that the work of Your mercy may spread throughout the whole world and that the Feast of The Divine Mercy may be solemnly promulgated and celebrated.

Secondly: that sinners, especially dying sinners, may have recourse to Your mercy and experience the unspeakable effects of this mercy.

Thirdly: that all the work of Your mercy may be realized according to Your wishes, and for a certain person who is in charge of this work. ...

Accept, most merciful Jesus, this, my inadequate sacrifice, which I offer to You today before heaven and earth. May Your Most Sacred Heart, so full of mercy, complete what is lacking in my offering, and offer it to Your Father for the conversion of sinners. I thirst after souls, O Christ (*Diary*, 1680).

Though we are not all called to suffer in the way St. Faustina did, suffering is part of all our lives — we are all suffering in some way. The challenge to us is to make use of it for others by offering with Christ whatever sufferings we endure, remembering the words of St. Paul: "It is your privilege to take Christ's part — not only to believe in Him, but also to suffer for Him" (Phil 1:29 NAB).

INTERCESSORY PRAYER

Pray perseveringly, be attentive to prayer, and pray in a spirit of thanksgiving. Pray for us, too, that God may provide an opening to proclaim the mystery of Christ, for which I am prisoner. Pray that I may speak it clearly, as I must (Col. 4:2-5, NAB).

In addition to interceding by offering her sufferings for others and intervening for those in need, St. Faustina prayed for others — prayer for others was, for her, a way of life. She prayed for the girls in the care of the convent, she prayed for the sick, for sinners, for priests, for her fellow sisters, for the Church, for her nation, and for the whole world. Throughout her *Diary*, we find a special concern for the miserable, the suffering, the dying, and the souls in purgatory.

There are a variety of ways to intercede for others, and St. Faustina exemplified many of them, providing us with a marvelous example of how to live out St. Paul's exhortation to intercede at all times, and with all sorts of prayers:

> Pray at all times in the Spirit, with all prayer and suppli-
> cation, to that end keep alert with all perseverance,
> making supplication for all the saints, and also for me ...
> (Eph 6:18-20 RSV).

Since St. Paul asked for prayers, even for himself, St. Faustina prayed regularly for our present day apostles: the pope, bishops, and priests. The clergy were her special charge. Often, this was very specific prayer for individual priests. Of one such instance she writes, "I saw a certain priest in need and prayed for him until Jesus looked upon him with kindness and granted him His strength (*Diary*, 986).

When the blood sister of St. Faustina came to her in darkness and despair, she took her into prayer:

> The good God entrusted her to my care, and for two
> weeks I was able to work with her. But how many
> sacrifices this soul cost me is known only to God. For
> no other soul did I bring so many sacrifices and suffer-
> ings and prayers before the throne of God as I did for
> her soul. I felt that I had forced God to grant her grace.
> When I reflect on all this, I see that it was truly a
> miracle. Now I can see how much power intercessory
> prayer has before God (*Diary*, 202).

"Forced God to grant her grace!" What a strong teaching this is! God wants us to compel Him to be merciful by offering constant prayer and sacrifices for others. He wants us to pray like Abraham and Moses, arguing with God; for as long as our hearts are right, our lips can be bold. Indeed, St. Faustina's boldness in interceding rivaled that of Abraham and Moses:

> During Holy Mass, I felt the closeness of the Lord in a special way. After Holy Communion, I turned my gaze with trust toward the Lord and told Him ... "Jesus, I beg You, by the inconceivable power of Your mercy, let all the souls who will die today escape the fire of hell, even if they have been the greatest sinners. Today is Friday, the memorial of Your bitter agony on the Cross; because Your mercy is inconceivable, the Angels will not be surprised at this" (*Diary*, *873*).

And because of her pure love of Him, the Lord answered her prayer:

> **You have come to know well the depths of My mercy. I will do what you ask, but unite yourself continually with My agonizing Heart and make reparation to My justice. Know that you have asked Me for a great thing, but I see that this was dictated by your pure love for Me; that is why I am complying with your requests** (*Diary*, 873).

St. Faustina also prayed for the girls in the care of the convent:

> I saw one of the wards offending God greatly by sins of impure thoughts. I also saw a certain person who was the cause of her sin. My soul was pierced with fear, and I asked God, for the sake of Jesus' pain, to snatch her from this terrible misery.
>
> Jesus answered that He would grant her that favor, not for her sake, but for the sake of my request. Now

I understood how much we ought to pray for sinners
... (*Diary*, 349-350).

Being made aware of someone dying in the need of
prayer, she would pray until she sensed that person was at
peace.

> + I felt today how greatly a certain dying soul desired
> prayers. I prayed until I felt she had died. Oh, dying
> souls are in such need of prayer! O Jesus, inspire
> souls to pray often for the dying (*Diary*, 1015).

She seemed to have a special gift of praying for the
dying, even when all external signs indicated no hope:

> I often attend upon the dying and through entreaties
> obtain for them trust in God's mercy, and I implore
> God for an abundance of divine grace, which is always
> victorious. God's mercy sometimes touches the sinner
> at the last moment, in a wondrous and mysterious way.
> Outwardly, it seems as if everything were lost, but it is
> not so. The soul, illumined by a ray of God's powerful
> final grace, turns to God in the last moment with such
> a power of love that, in an instant, it receives from God
> forgiveness of sin and punishment, while outwardly it
> shows no sign either of repentance or of contrition,
> because souls [at that stage] no longer react to external
> things (*Diary*, 1698).

The souls in purgatory were especially thankful for her
intercessory prayer:

> When the soul of a certain young lady came to me
> one night, she made me aware of her presence, and
> made known to me that she needed my prayer. I
> prayed for a while, but her spirit did not leave me.
> Then I thought to myself, "If you are a good spirit,
> leave me in peace, and the indulgences I will gain
> tomorrow will be for you." At that moment, the

spirit left my room, and I recognized that she was in purgatory (*Diary*, 1723).

From these entries, and from many other entries in her *Diary*, we learn that St. Faustina prayed in a variety of ways: offering her sufferings, reciting the Chaplet of The Divine Mercy and the Rosary of Our Lady, making novenas, repeating ejaculations and praying litanies. But her presence to God in a deep union of love was the basis of her intercession. She knew the Lord and loved Him so intimately that when she asked, she knew she would receive. For her, prayer was a cooperative partnership with the Lord and Our Lady. Like Mary, she shared in the suffering of the cross, and thus shared in its power as the source of mercy on the world.

PROCLAIMING MERCY PREPARES FOR HIS COMING AGAIN

He will come again to judge the living and the dead (Apostles Creed).

Each year during the season of Advent, the Liturgy of the Eucharist and the Liturgy of the Hours gradually increase the Church's cry and yearning: "Come, Lord Jesus!" Over and over again we are admonished to "be prepared; get ready; He is near!"

Some hard facts must be considered in this matter of the coming of The Lord. We have too easily interpreted away the fact of His coming, and we live as though it had no reality. We need to accept, in a real way, *that* Jesus Christ is coming again. This is a fact of our faith. We profess it in the Creed at Mass (Nicene Creed), we proclaim it in every Eucharist, and we pray for it in every Our Father — "Your kingdom come!"

We need to live as though He were coming immediately, and we need to prepare ourselves by watching, waiting, and praying. This is the gospel teaching (see Mt 24; Mk 13; Lk 21).

When He is coming we do not know — that knowledge is reserved for the Father — but we do know that He will come in glory upon the clouds, and we must be ready to greet Him at whatever hour He comes. We may wonder why the Lord is slow in coming, but there are clear indications in the Sacred Scripture (see 2 Thes 2; 1 Cor 15:25; 2 Pet 3:8-13) that the delay is due to us — not the Lord.

The Lord specifically told St. Faustina that He is waiting for us:

> **I am prolonging the time of mercy for the sake of** [sinners]. **But woe to them if they do not recognize this time of My visitation** (*Diary*, 1160).

We can hasten the day of the coming of the Lord by leading holy lives, by being merciful, and by standing firm against Satan. The Lord is waiting for us to do just that. He wants to show mercy on us all since He wants none to perish, but wants all to come to repentance. He wants, generation after generation, to receive His mercy (see 1 Pet 5:6-11; 2 Pet 3:9, 11-13; Rom 11:32).

Through St. Faustina, our Lord promised a sign before His coming as the Just Judge — a sign that recalls the promise of Scripture (see Lk 21:25; Mt 24:29; Mk 13:24):

> **Write this: Before I come as the Just Judge, I am coming first as the King of Mercy. Before the day of justice arrives, there will be given to people a sign in the heavens of this sort:**
>
> **All light in the heavens will be extinguished, and there will be great darkness over the whole earth. Then the sign of the cross will be seen in the sky, and from the openings where the hands and the feet of the Savior were nailed will come forth**

great lights which will light up the earth for a period of time. This will take place shortly before the last day (*Diary*, 83).

But a more general sign of His coming is His mercy itself:

Speak to the world about My mercy; let all mankind recognize My unfathomable mercy. It is a sign for the end times; after it will come the day of justice (*Diary*, 848).

The times we live in are a time to turn to the mercy of God. This is the day of mercy before His coming as Judge of justice. Now is the time to turn to His mercy, so that He might crush the head of Satan, purify us from our sins, and place death itself beneath His feet. Now is the time to proclaim God's mercy.

The call of St. Faustina to a mission of proclaiming God's mercy is a very special one for our times:

Today I heard the words: **In the Old Covenant I sent prophets wielding thunderbolts to my people. Today I am sending you with My mercy to the people of the whole world. I do not want to punish aching mankind, but I desire to heal it, pressing it to My Merciful Heart. I use punishment when they themselves force Me to do so; My hand is reluctant to take hold of the sword of justice. Before the Day of Justice, I am sending the Day of Mercy** (*Diary*, 1588).

On a number of occasions, Our Lady appeared to St. Faustina with revelations that echo the urgency of those of La Salette, Lourdes, Fatima, and now allegedly at Medjugorje. One special appearance stands out. On the feast of the Annunciation, March 25, 1936, Our Lady said to St. Faustina:

I gave the Savior to the world; as for you, you have to speak to the world of His great mercy and prepare the

*world for the Second Coming of Him who will come, not
as a merciful Savior, but as a just Judge. Oh, how terrible
is that day! Determined is the day of justice, the day of
divine wrath. The angels tremble before it. Speak to souls
about this great mercy while it is still time for [granting]
mercy. If you keep silent now, you will be answering for a
great number of souls on that terrible day (Diary, 635).*

This ties in with the preaching and writings of Pope John
Paul II. In his first encyclical, *Redemptor Hominis,* and again
in his encyclical *Dominum et Vivificantem,* he referred to the
year 2001 as the "new Advent." He asked:

What should we do in order that this new Advent of
the Church connected with the approaching end of
the second millennium may bring us closer to him
whom Sacred Scripture calls "Everlasting Father?" It
is certain that the Church of the new Advent, the
Church that is continually preparing for the new
coming of the Lord, must be the Church of the
Eucharist and of Penance.

John Paul seemed to have a mystic sense about the new
Advent and the beginning of the third millennium as a time
of Eucharist and mercy!

We can think of the third millennium in light of what St.
Peter said: "In the Lord's eyes, one day is as a thousand years
and a thousand years are as a day" (2 Pet 3:8). It would mean
that we are but entering the "third day," which is the day of
resurrection for the Church now in travail, the day of the
glorious reign of the Lord with His purified Church!

Jesus is waiting for us to be merciful, even as our Father
is merciful (see Lk 6:36 RSV). Like St. Faustina we, too, are
to proclaim God's mercy — by word and action:

**Souls who spread the honor of My mercy I shield
through their entire life as a tender mother her
infant, and at the hour of death I will not be a judge
for them, but the Merciful Savior (*Diary,* 1075).**

With St. Faustina, we should encourage priests to proclaim God's mercy in preparation for the Lord's coming again:

> **Tell My priests that hardened sinners will repent on hearing their words, when they will speak about My unfathomable mercy, about the compassion I have for them in My Heart. To priests who proclaim and extol My mercy, I will give wondrous power, I will anoint their words and touch the hearts of those to whom they will speak** (*Diary*, 1521).

Together, we can proclaim His mercy and hasten the day of His coming.

MARY, THE MOTHER OF MERCY

I am not only the Queen of Heaven, but also the Mother of Mercy and your Mother (*Diary*, 330).

I am Mother to you all, thanks to the unfathomable mercy of God (*Diary*, 449).

These words of Our Lady echo the words of our Lord from the cross when He explicitly extended the maternity of His mother to include all of us:

> When Jesus saw His mother and the disciple whom He loved standing near, He said to His mother, "Woman, behold your son!" Then He said to the disciple, "Behold, your mother!" (Jn 19:25-27 RSV).

The Second Vatican Council made it clear to us that Mary is our mother as well as the Mother of God, and that her maternity continues in heaven as she *cares* for us:

In an utterly singular way, she cooperated by her
obedience, faith, hope, and burning charity in the
Savior's work of restoring supernatural life to souls.
For this reason, she is a *mother to us* in the order of
grace ... for, taken up to heaven, she did not lay aside
this saving role, but by her manifold acts of intercession, continues to win for us gifts of eternal salvation.
By her maternal charity, Mary cares for the brethren
of her son ... (*Lumen Gentium*, 61-62).

As we look at Mary's role in the life of St. Faustina, we
need to keep in mind that Mary is also our mother and that
she wants to care for us, teach us, and prepare us for our
mission of mercy.

In a very special way, St. Faustina experienced Mary as
her mother. On the feast of The Immaculate Conception, Our
Lady said to her:

"*My daughter, at God's command I am to be, in a
special and exclusive way, your Mother; but I desire that
you, too, in a special way be my child*" (*Diary*, 1414).

Then followed the mother's instruction. As mother,
Mary wanted St. Faustina to model her most characteristic
virtues: humility, purity, and love of God:

*I desire, my dearly beloved daughter, that you practice the
three virtues that are the dearest to me — and most
pleasing to God. The first is humility, humility, and once
again humility. The second virtue, purity; the third
virtue, love of God. As my daughter, you must especially
radiate with these virtues* (*Diary*, 1415).

At the time of the renewal of her vows as a religious, St.
Faustina received a special gift of purity of heart, mind, and
body, which she attributed to the intercession of Mary:

Jesus appeared suddenly at my side in a white
garment with a golden girdle around His waist, and

He said to me, **I give you eternal love that your purity may be untarnished and as a sign that you will never be subject to temptations against purity**. Jesus took off His golden cincture and tied it around my waist.

Since then I have never experienced any attacks against this virtue, either in my heart or in my mind. I later understood that this was one of the greatest graces which the Most Holy Virgin Mary had obtained for me, as for many years I had been asking this grace of her (*Diary*, 40).

Saint Faustina then goes on to record the resulting increase of devotion to the Mother of God and how she taught her to love God:

Since that time, I have experienced an increasing devotion to the Mother of God. She has taught me how to love God interiorly and also how to carry out His holy will in all things, O Mary, You are joy, because through you God descended to earth [and] into my heart (*Diary*, 40).

Saint Faustina honored her Mother Mary in prayer, offering herself to Mary. This gift of herself to Mary is a consecration — that Mary would be her mother and protectress in all situations:

O Mary, my Mother and my Lady, I give you my soul, my body, my life and my death, and all that will follow it. I place everything in your hands. O Mother, cover my soul with your virginal mantle and grant me the grace of purity of heart, soul and body. Defend me with your power against all enemies, and especially against those who hide their malice behind the mask of virtue ... (*Diary*, 79).

Mary became her instructress, ever teaching her how to live for God (see *Diary*, 620). From Mary, she learned how to love even in the midst of suffering and how to offer her suffering for others.

> The Mother of God told me to do what she had done, that, even when joyful, I should always keep my eyes fixed on the cross, and she told me that the graces God was granting me were not for me alone, but for other souls as well (*Diary*, 561).

She learned, too, the need for intercessory prayer. In words echoing the message at Fatima, Mary explained to her:

> *My daughter, what I demand from you is prayer, prayer, and once again, prayer ...* (*Diary*, 325).

In thus teaching St. Faustina how to intercede for mercy through suffering and prayer, Mary was showing her how to carry out her mission to prepare the world for the Second Coming of the Lord. And she now wants to instruct you and me for our mission of mercy to prepare for the Lord's Coming again.

This kind of preparation and instructions by Mary takes time, commitment, and prayer. For St. Faustina, the preparation extended over her lifetime, but there was a special moment at the Shrine of Our Lady of Jasna Gora during her first visit to Czestochowa. She prayed for an extended time; renewed her vows of poverty, celibacy, and obedience; and listened and talked to her mother as a child.

> I saw the Mother of God [image] for the first time, when I went to attend the unveiling of the image at five in the morning. I prayed without interruption until eleven, and it seemed to me that I had just come. The superior of the house there sent a sister for me, to tell me to come to breakfast, and said she was worried that I would miss my train. The Mother of God told me many things. I entrusted my perpetual vows to her. I felt that I was her child and that she was my mother. She did not refuse any of my requests (*Diary*, 260).

Mary is our Mother, and we are her children.

EPILOGUE
Divine Mercy — The Answer
To The Troubled World

On the evening TV news, there was yet another disturbing and very visual report on AIDS, followed by a terrifying report on bombing in Lebanon. The other day, a woman came seeking help in dealing with the death of her young son, who had committed suicide. Another came, torn apart by the knowledge that her teenage daughter is pregnant and is planning an abortion. And so the litany of evil born of sin goes on and on — wars, division, divorce, crime, terrorism, poverty, famine — all overshadowed by the threat of annihilation of the world. The situation makes a father of a family dread raising his children in this sick and dying society. What should the proper response be?

In the Church, too, we are experiencing confusion as we hear of theologians and priests teaching sexual morality in opposition to the teaching of the Church — condoning artificial birth control, abortion, and homosexual activity. We are scandalized as we read of priests in jail for homosexual abuse of boys. We are disturbed by angry demonstrations fostering the ordination of women. We are shocked and saddened by public disagreement and vicious criticism of Pope Benedict XVI.

What parents want to send their children to a Catholic college that teaches this kind of confusion? Within the Church, we now have a plurality of infallibility! The Church has been invaded by the secularism of the world. What is the Christian response?

All too often, our human response is negative — we so easily become part of the problem by viewing this world as the end of it all. We respond to reports of increased crime and terrorism by fear and anxiety, and we grow in unrest, as we put new locks on the doors or raid the refrigerator. We find people to blame, and we focus on them our growing feelings of frustration, anger, and even hatred.

We see a man on the street, dazed by alcohol or drugs, and with a look of disgust, we cross the street to avoid him. To cope with the tension of a broken family or the unpleasantness at work, we take more tranquilizers or watch another movie on TV. We become more and more critical, more and more apathetic.

These human responses of fear, anger, hate, escape, denial, and despair are all just ways of "cursing the darkness." They are useless, and they make things worse, because they are not Christian responses prompted by faith, hope, and love. They are worldly responses prompted by an acceptance of worldly values. When we curse the darkness, we become part of it.

Even when we manage to be more positive in our responses — reaching out to out neighbors, giving an encouraging word, helping with food and shelter, or even just listening — it doesn't seem enough.

We know these things are good and must be continued, but how are they changing the world situation? What effect can I have on world morality by trying to convince my children not to watch sexually explicit movies or view immoral images on the Internet? How can I counter the influence of worldly theologians by my own efforts to remain true to Church teachings? How am I really helping to foster world peace by being pleasant to the people I meet? Sure, "if everyone lit just one candle," it would make a difference; but in my heart I know that everyone won't, and in such a darkness, what good is my little candle?

Our positive human responses are necessary; but, in themselves, they are not enough. They need to be conformed and united to God's infinite response, thus bringing God's sovereign action into the world — allowing God, through us, to bless the darkness with His light.

What is God's response to the present situation in the Church and the world? Perhaps it is similar to His reaction to evil in the days of Noah:

When the Lord saw how great was man's wickedness on earth, and how no desire that his heart conceived was ever anything but evil, he regretted that he had made man on the earth and his heart was grieved (Gen 6:5-6 NAB).

But Noah found favor in God's sight, and for his sake, God saved the human race and creation through the wood of an Ark — a great prefiguring of our salvation through the Holy one of God, Jesus Christ, who saved us by the wood of the cross.

Today, we need to turn to the ark of salvation that God has provided for us — His infinite mercy! His mercy is like an ocean of love that is bottomless and limitless — always available for sinners trapped in evil, always capable of cleansing, healing, and transforming even the greatest of sinners, always reaching out to all of us.

Pope John Paul II identified the problem in the Church and the world as "lack of peace"; and he proclaimed that the response of the Church to this problem is the *mercy of God* — the *only* answer. He challenged the Church not only to preach and practice mercy, but to *implore God's mercy* (see *Rich in Mercy*, 15). Describing the evil of our day in terms of Noah, he encouraged us to call upon the "motherly" love of God:

Like the prophets, let us appeal to that love which has maternal characteristics — which like a mother goes after each of her children, after each lost sheep, even if the lost are in the millions, even if the evil in the world outweighs honesty, even if mankind deserves because of its sins a kind of modern "flood," as did the generation of Noah.

He exhorted us also to cry to the *Father's love* revealed in Jesus, the source of mercy:

Let us then appeal also to that kind of fatherly love revealed to us by Christ in His messianic mission, which reached its ultimate expression in His cross, in His passion and in His Resurrection!

In this cry for mercy, Mary is to be our model: Let us appeal to God through Christ, mindful of the words of Mary's *Magnificat* which proclaims "mercy from age to age."

Let us cry out to God's own mercy for this present generation!

May the Church, which like Mary continues to be the spiritual mother of humankind, express in this prayer her total maternal concern, as well as that trusting love from which is born the most burning need for prayer.

This appeal for mercy is love — love for God, whom modern man has rejected by his atheism and materialism; love for God, whose response to this rejection is forgiveness:

This cry for mercy is at the same time an expression of our love of God from whom modern man has distanced himself and made of Him a stranger, proclaiming in various ways that he doesn't "need" God.

This then is mercy, the *love of God* whose insult — rejection by modern man — we feel deeply and are ready to cry out with Christ on the cross, "Father, forgive them, for they do not know what they do" (Lk 23:34 RSV).

It is also love for all mankind — each and every one of us:

This cry for mercy is love for all people, the care which ensures for everyone all true good, and removes and drives away every sort of evil (*Rich in Mercy*, VIII:15).

Divine Mercy is the only answer to the problems of the world — there is no escape from that answer!

This message given to us by our Lord through our Holy Father of beloved memory is the same message we receive through the revelations to St. Faustina:

Mankind will have no peace until it turns with trust to My mercy (*Diary*, 300).

The essence of the devotion to The Divine Mercy — trust and mercy, expressed by word, deed, and prayer — is also the essence of the answer to problems in the Church and in the world. We are to be channels of His mercy to the world. We are to be merciful as the heavenly Father is merciful (see Lk 6:36), and so find favor with God, even as Noah did, thus cooperating in the salvation of this present age.

How are we to be channels of mercy? By the practice of trust and mercy in the face of every sinful and evil situation we encounter. We can respond to the situation in the Church and world by our acts of mercy and by imploring mercy — *not cursing* the darkness, but *blessing* it with the mercy of God.

When my heart is heavy over a theological teaching or doctrine not in keeping with the Church, I can cry out, "Jesus, mercy!" When my mind is confused when a priest criticizes the Church and then leaves the priesthood, I can intercede like St. Faustina and offer the pain in union with the Eucharistic sacrifice of Jesus for mercy on him. When my heart is crushed by the anguish of a broken marriage or rebellious children, I can grab hold of that deep pain — not denying or hiding from it — and cry out, "Come, Holy Spirit, purify and transform this brokenness. Come, Lord Jesus, forgive us!"

These acts and cries for mercy may seem like little insignificant acts, but these are the very acts God asks of us — these are the humble acts God asked of His own mother, Mary, and of St. Faustina. God asks us to follow the way of humility, the way He chose for His Son, Jesus.

Like St. Faustina, we, too, are invited to make use of the great channels of mercy: the Sacraments of Eucharist and Reconciliation, the works of mercy, and prayer to The Divine Mercy.

This kind of response to the situation in the Church and the world calls for trust in the Lord — a radical, total trust — that He is God, He is in charge, and He cares and loves us with an everlasting love.

The urgent need for this kind of response is the whole message of this book, a message that can be summarized in a few sentences:

Mankind will have no peace until it turns with trust to My mercy (*Diary*, 300).

JESUS, MERCY (see Lk 17:14).

"Blessed are the merciful, for they shall obtain mercy" (Mt 5:7).

O Blood and Water,
which gushed forth from the Heart of Jesus
as a fount of mercy for us,
I trust in You (*Diary*, 84).

Now is the time for mercy!

APPENDIX
The Importance
of Private Revelation

The revelations of our Lord to St. Faustina are classified by the Church as "private revelation."

There have been a number of other private revelations throughout the history of the Church; such as the revelations to St. Margaret Mary Alacoque (between 1673 and 1675) on the Sacred Heart of Jesus, and the revelations of Our Lady at Fatima (1917).

Some people don't seem to understand the value and significance of private revelations, even those approved by the Church. This attitude is often expressed in such statements as, "Oh, its only a private revelation." "I don't need another private revelation." "That's not for me." "I have problems with devotions and shrines."

Unfortunately, such attitudes are real obstacles to hearing the word of the Lord and of Our Lady.

A clear statement of the Church's attitude toward private revelation was made by Pope John Paul II in his homily at Fatima on May 13, 1982. Quoting the Second Vatican Council, he applied its teaching to the Fatima revelations:

> The Church has always taught and continues to proclaim that God's revelation was brought to completion in Jesus Christ, who is the fullness of that revelation, and that "no new public revelation is to be expected before the glorious manifestation of our Lord" (*Dei Verbum* 4). The Church evaluates and judges private revelations by the criterion of conformity with that single Revelation.

If the Church has accepted the message of Fatima, it
is above all because the message contains a truth and
a call whose basic content is the truth and the call of
the gospel itself.

"Repent, and believe in the gospel" (Lk 1:15): these
are the first words that the Messiah addressed to
humanity. The message of Fatima is, in its basic nucleus,
a call to conversion and repentance as in the Gospel.

Here, in a few words, John Paul II outlined the place of
private revelations — they reflect "the truth and the call of
the gospel."

The message of The Divine Mercy — Jesus Himself — is at
the heart of the gospel. It presents the truth and the call of the
gospel to our present age, and it was proclaimed by Pope John
Paul II, in his encyclical *Rich in Mercy*, as the message of our age.

The Church of our time ... must become more
particularly and profoundly conscious of the need to
bear witness in her whole mission to God's mercy, following in the footsteps of the tradition of the Old and
New Covenant, and above all of Jesus Christ Himself
and His apostles (VII, Introduction).

... the Church must consider it one of her principle
duties — at every stage of history and especially in
our modern age — *to proclaim and to introduce in
life* the mystery of mercy, supremely revealed in Jesus
Christ (#134).

God did not stop speaking to His people with the death
of the last apostle, John the beloved disciple. Public revelation
was completed with John's death, but God continues to speak
to us today.

Bishop Graber of Regensburg, addressing the Fatima
Congress at Freiburg, Germany, September 23, 1973, makes
this very clear:

Once again we affirm that revelation ended with Christ and His Apostles. But does that mean that God has to remain silent, that He can no longer speak to His elect? Does it mean, as some believers think, that He should remain apart and leave the world abandoned to itself? Would not this be a very strange kind of God indeed! Did He not expressly say through His prophet that He would "pour forth of His Spirit on all flesh, that sons and daughters would prophesy, that old men would have visions in dreams? Even upon servants and handmaids He would pour forth on His Spirit (see Acts 2:17; Jn 3:1-5). Is such prophecy to be limited only to the first Pentecost? Certainly not (Quoted in *Fatima: The Great Sign*, Francis Johnston, A.M.I., Washington, NJ 07882).

In the article "Theology of Devotion to the Sacred Heart," found in *Theological Investigations* (Vol. III, pp. 338, 339), Fr. Karl Rahner, SJ, explains that, while private revelations do not offer new doctrine for belief, they do provide extraordinary guidance for the Church, emphasizing specific and urgent ways of putting faith into action. They present us with God's evaluation of what is most needed at particular times.

To this, Fr. Walter Kern, in his *Updated Devotion to the Sacred Heart*, adds an important consideration. He explains that private revelations.

> ... are offered as a special grace for the good of men in general. One can save his or her soul without every special grace from God, but the fact that God offered it, because it is or was useful, must weigh heavily in one's judgment of it.

Especially in times of travail, like ours, we need to hear the word of the Lord proclaimed clearly and forcefully like a clear trumpet. "If the bugle's sound is uncertain, who will get ready for the battle?" (1 Cor 14:8). Who will be able to listen and act? Who will be able to say with Samuel, "Speak, Lord, for Your servant is listening" (1 Sam 3:9)?

STEPS TOWARD A THEOLOGY OF THE IMAGE OF THE DIVINE MERCY

The image of Jesus, The Divine Mercy, as He revealed Himself to St. Faustina, is an image that capsulizes the paschal mystery. Each of the major paschal feasts is portrayed in this one icon of Jesus entering the cenacle, the upper room, where so many mysteries took place.

The white robe brings to mind Jesus as High Priest. On *Holy Thursday*, He ordains His apostles as priests, and institutes the Holy Eucharist. In the cenacle, as the Eternal High Priest He offers His passion and death to be fulfilled the next day. As High Priest, He prays: "I consecrate Myself for their sakes now that they may be consecrated in truth" (Jn 17:19).

The wounds in His hands and feet and His pierced side remind us of the saving events of *Good Friday*: the insulting trials, the scourging, the crowning with thorns, the crucifixion, the soldier's lance thrust into His side, and the burial in the tomb. Now the wounds are the signs of the victory that wrought our salvation.

The brilliant rays of red and pale light coming from the area of His Heart bring to mind the resurrected Christ appearing to His apostles in the cenacle. We see Jesus on *Easter Sunday* night, radiant in glory, bringing His blessing of victory and peace as He breathes the Holy Spirit upon them for the power to forgive sins. The apostles are filled with joy that overcomes their fears.

Again, on the *octave day of Easter*, we see Jesus entering the cenacle, and this time Thomas is with them. The very presence of the risen Lord evokes the great profession of Thomas' faith: 'My Lord and my God" (Jn 20:28). And further, the response of Thomas is the occasion of the encouraging words of Jesus: "Blessed are those who have not seen and yet believe" (Jn 20:29). This profession of Thomas on the octave day of the Resurrection is the culmination of the Gospel according to St. John.

The image of Jesus, The Divine Mercy, with His hand raised in blessing, recalls the blessing of the *Ascension* and His continued intercession: "... lifting up His hands He blessed them. While He blessed them, He parted from them and was carried up into heaven," (Lk 24:50-51) where He now lives to make intercession for us at the right hand of the Father (see Heb 7:25 and Eph 1:19-21).

The resplendent red and pale rays of the image, representing the blood and water that gushed from the pierced Heart of Jesus, also represent the fire of the Holy Spirit coming upon the assembled disciples with Mary on the *Day of Pentecost*. The Church is born by the water, the blood, and the Holy Spirit — and these three are one (see 1 Jn 5-6).

This image of Jesus, The Divine Mercy, is not only a capsulization of the various feasts of the paschal mystery, but is also the summation of the Feast of Mercy. It is this image that our Lord asked St. Faustina to have blessed and venerated on the octave day of Easter.

It is this image that our Lord asked to be signed: "Jesus, I trust in You!" and venerated as a vessel to draw grace from the fount of mercy. It is a visual reminder of all that Jesus did for us through the paschal mystery and of what He asks of us in return — to trust Him and be merciful to others.

STEPS TOWARD A THEOLOGY OF THE CHAPLET OF THE DIVINE MERCY

... how much more shall the blood of Christ, who through the eternal spirit offered Himself without blemish to God, purify your conscience from dead works to serve the living God (Heb 9:14 RSV).

The Chaplet of The Divine Mercy is a prayer that arises out of Sacred Scripture and the ancient tradition of the Church. Yet it is a new prayer that combines, in a powerful way, every element of the prayer of the Church for mercy. Each part of the chaplet reflects this combination of Sacred Scripture, tradition, and powerful pleading for mercy.

"Eternal Father ..."

We begin by addressing God the Father, the Creator, whom Jesus revealed as a Father rich in mercy (see Eph 2:4), and whom He taught us to call "Abba."

... I offer You the Body and Blood, Soul and Divinity ..."

Our prayer is an offering to the Father through the eternal Spirit of Jesus, His beloved Son, true God and true man (see Heb 9:14).

The words "Body and Blood, Soul and Divinity" describe the presence of the Lord Jesus in the Eucharist, and they recall the catechism definition of Eucharist as inspired by the Council of Trent.

By this offering to the Father, we extend the Eucharist to each moment. We, as a priestly people, are instructed by the Church through the Second Vatican Council that both priests and laity "... should give thanks to God; by offering the Immaculate Victim" (Liturgy, 48).

By this Eucharistic offering we can unite ourselves with Christ present now in all the tabernacles of the world. We can also unite our offering with the merits of Christ's sacrifice on the cross.

This offering echoes the prayer of the Angel at Fatima as he prostrated himself before the Blessed Sacrament:

> O Most Holy Trinity, Father, Son and Holy Spirit, I adore You profoundly. I offer You the Most Precious Body, Blood, Soul and Divinity of Jesus Christ present in all the tabernacles of the world, in reparation for the outrages, sacrileges and indifference by which He is offended. By the infinite merits of the Sacred Heart of Jesus and the Immaculate Heart of Mary, I beg the conversion of poor sinners.

"... of Your dearly beloved Son ..."

By these words, we echo the words of the Father at the transfiguration of Jesus. "This is my beloved Son, with whom I am well pleased; listen to Him" (Mt 17:5 RSV) By this offering we return to the Father His most precious gift — His own Son — given to us. "For God so loved the world that He gave His only Son ..." (Jn 3:16 RSV).

"... Our Lord Jesus Christ ..."

This triple title of Jesus, frequently used by St. Paul (e.g., 2 Cor 1:3) in his letters, is a summary of the Gospel, and a key to who Jesus is. When we say, "Lord," we mean that Jesus is the Lord God who reigns at the right hand of the Father and who "will come again to judge the living and the dead" (Apostles Creed). When we say, "Jesus," we mean Savior. It is He who has saved us by the Passion and death He suffered in His human body. And when we say, "Christ," we mean anointed. He was the one anointed by the Holy Spirit to do the works of the Father, was raised from the dead by that Spirit, and is the source of that same Spirit for us.

"... in atonement for our sins and those of the whole world

This offering of the chaplet prayer is an expiation for everyone, for all our sins. It is a beautiful echo of the words of St. John:

> He is the atoning sacrifice for our sins, and not only for ours but also for the sins of the whole world (1 Jn 2:2 NIV).

"For the sake of His sorrowful Passion ..."

We implore the Father to look at the Passion of His Son — the scourging, the crowning with thorns, the ridicule and insults, the bitter pain of His crucifixion and, above all, the anguish of His Heart. The Passion of Jesus Christ is the perfect act of obedience and trust, offered "through the eternal Spirit."

"... have mercy on us and on the whole world."

For the sake of His Passion, we implore the Father for mercy, because mercy is the great plan of God for all mankind. St. Paul describes God's desire:

> For God has consigned all men to disobedience, that he may have mercy upon all (Rom 11:32 RSV).

He then breaks out into a hymn to describe this plan:

> O the depth of the riches and wisdom and knowledge of God! How unsearchable are His judgments and how inscrutable His ways! (Rom 11:33 RSV).

The Passion, death, and Resurrection of Jesus is the source of mercy, of atonement, and of eternal life for all who trust and believe.

"Holy God, Holy Mighty One, Holy Immortal One ..."

The chaplet concludes with the repetition of the great doxology of the Byzantine Church, honoring the Most Holy

Trinity: the Father, the Son, and the Holy Spirit. The Father is the Holy God and Father of all. The Son is the Mighty One who saved us and did the works of the Father by the power of the Holy Spirit. The Holy Spirit, the Immortal One, is the Everliving Lord God, "the giver of life" (Nicene Creed).

This concluding part of the chaplet also echoes Sacred Scripture in the prophet Isaiah: "Holy, holy, holy is the Lord of hosts; the whole earth is full of his glory" (Is 6:3 RSV); and again, "For thus says He who is high and exalted, living eternally, whose name is the Holy One" (Is 57:15); and in the prophet Habakkuk, "Are You not from eternity, O Lord, my holy God, immortal?" (Hab 1:12 NAB).

And then, at the end of the concluding prayer, a final echo of the great plea for this Holy, Mighty, and Immortal God to fulfill His loving plan:

"... have mercy on us and on the whole world."

STEPS TOWARD A THEOLOGY OF THE FEAST OF THE DIVINE MERCY

Pope John Paul II's establishment of the Feast of The Divine Mercy on the octave day of Easter has fulfilled the purpose of the restoration of the liturgical year, allowing "the faithful through their faith, hope, and love, to share more deeply in the 'whole mystery of Christ as it unfolds throughout the year'" (*Moto Proprio* of Pope Paul VI, 1969, on the Liturgical Year and Roman Calendar, quoting Vatican II on the *Liturgy*, 102). It would insure even greater prominence to the paschal mystery of Christ, so that the faithful could more effectively "lay hold of the mysteries of Christ and be filled with his saving grace" (ibid.)

How has it achieved these purposes? In a number of ways. The Feast of Mercy has its roots deeply planted in the Old and New Testament and in the early Church Tradition. It is a feast with three distinct dimensions, each emphasizing an aspect of the paschal mystery that needs to be brought out more clearly and appropriated by the faithful: merciful love, atonement, and covenant.

The Feast of Mercy as a Celebration and Summation of God's Merciful Love

The Triduum of Holy Week, along with the entire Easter season, focuses on various aspects of the paschal mystery. Holy Thursday celebrates the Mass of the Chrism and the evening Mass of the Mandatum — the washing of the feet of the disciples, ordination to the priesthood, the institution of the Eucharist, and the last discourse of our Lord promising the sending of the Holy Spirit. Good Friday commemorates the Passion and death of Jesus on the cross. The Easter vigil, the pinnacle of the paschal mystery, celebrates the fulfillment of the prophecies of the Redeemer who is our light and salvation, bringing us new life by water and the Holy Spirit. The Easter season continues this celebration, leading to the Ascension of the Lord and to Pentecost — the fulfillment of the promise to send the Holy Spirit.

The Feast of Mercy focuses on God's mercy as an event! It focuses on God's continuing action of mercy throughout salvation history as we see it recorded in the Letter to the Romans, chapter 9, 10, 11, culminating in His loving plan to have mercy on all! (see Rom 11:32). This feast is the summation of the whole paschal mystery, capsulizing the grace in the celebration of the event of His mercy active in our lives now. It is because of His mercy that we have forgiveness of sin and new life as children of God. This needs to be celebrated!

The Feast of Mercy as a Day of Atonement

The Feast of Mercy is the fulfillment of the Old Testament Day of Atonement (see Lv 16, Lv 23:26-32, and Sir 50). It is a day of forgiveness of sins for those who approach the Eucharist and the Sacrament of Reconciliation. It is an annual celebration like the Day of Atonement — all sins and punishment are washed away in God's infinite mercy. The focus of this paschal event is on God's mercy for us sinners and His free gift to those who turn to Him with trust.

Interestingly enough, the texts of the liturgy of that Sunday focus on the forgiveness of sins. The Gospel is of Jesus appearing in the upper room and bestowing the authority to forgive sins (see Jn 20:19-51), and the other readings are also on mercy (see Ps 118 and 1 Pet 1:3-9).

Our Easter liturgy fulfills the major feasts of the Old Testament — Passover and Pentecost — and was only missing the Day of Atonement. This Feast of Mercy now completes the needed fulfillment of Old Testament feasts.

The Feast of Mercy as the Covenant of Mercy

The octave day has its roots in the Old Testament and New Testament as the Day of Covenant. On the eighth day after his birth, a male child was circumcised as a sign of the covenant and given his name (see Gen 17:12-14; see also Lk 2:21 for the circumcision of Jesus).

In the early Church, the newly baptized, newly born in Christ, wore white robes until the Sunday in White (*Dominica in Albis)* the octave day of Easter, symbolizing their innocence. The Feast of Mercy once again celebrates the white innocence we receive by the Covenant of Mercy.

St. Augustine calls these days "days of mercy and pardon" (Sermon 156, *Dom. in Albis*) and the Sunday "the compendium of the days of mercy." And then, referring to the setting aside of the white robes, he warns, "Let not our interior purity be lessened as we set aside its exterior symbols" (156 on *Dom. in Albis*).

Like the covenant of Sinai we, too, prepare for the Feast by purification from our sins and by the sprinkling of blood and proclaiming of the law (Ex 19:14-15, Ex 24:6-8) — but this time we are cleansed by the precious Blood of the Lord and the proclamation of His mercy.

On the octave day of Easter we, too, need to ratify the Covenant of Mercy, reaffirming not only our Baptism, already renewed at the Easter vigil, but also the Sacraments of Reconciliation, Confirmation, and Eucharist.

Interestingly enough, all the elements of creation are structured in units of eight, as seen in the periodic table, and musical chords resonate with the octave.

The Feast of Mercy as the octave day of the Resurrection strikes the resonant chord of Easter, developing the meaning and richness of the paschal mystery and applying it in a new and deeper way. It resonates with all of nature, sounding anew the grace of the Resurrection, alleluia!

The Feast of Mercy — the Desire of the Lord

As we have seen, the reasons for establishing the Feast of Mercy are strong and clear in themselves. This feast is rooted in the Old and New Testament, and an earlier form of the feast was celebrated from the fourth century as Dominica in Albis. But, in our times, there is an additional reason that made the need for the Feast of Mercy even more urgent, and that strengthens the meaning and effectiveness of such a feast for the faithful. In a series of reported revelations to St. Faustina Kowalska, our Lord specifically and repeatedly asked that the Feast of Mercy be established on the octave day of Easter.

All the Elements of the Message and Devotion to The Divine Mercy Focus on the Feast of Mercy

In preparation for the Feast of Mercy, we are asked, through St. Faustina, to make a novena of chaplets to The Divine Mercy and to be purified by the Sacrament of Reconciliation. Priests are asked to proclaim the mercy of God. The image of Jesus, the Merciful Savior, is to be blessed and venerated as a reminder to trust in Jesus and do works of mercy. And we are to renew, ratify, and seal the covenant of mercy by receiving Holy Communion.

The Desired fulfillment: a Deeper Sharing

Those who have been celebrating the octave of Easter in this way, as the Feast of Mercy, have experienced the desired effect of the Second Vatican Council for the liturgical year renewal — a deeper share in the mystery of Christ.

CHRONOLOGY OF EVENTS

The main events of the life of St. Faustina Kowalska, her cause of beatification and canonization, and her ongoing mission of mercy in our time:

AUGUST 25, 1905: Sister Faustina is born Helen Kowalska in the village of Glogowiec, near Lodz, Poland.

1912: At the age of seven, Helen hears for the first time a voice in her soul, calling her to a more perfect way of life.

JUNE 19-25, 1925: At the age of 20, during the Octave of Corpus Christi, Helen makes a vow of perpetual chastity.

AUGUST 1, 1925: Helen is accepted into the Congregation of the Sisters of Our Lady of Mercy as a lay sister. She begins her postulancy at Warsaw and then leaves for Krakow to complete it.

APRIL 30, 1926: Helen begins her two-year novitiate in Krakow, receiving her religious habit and the name Maria Faustina.

FEBRUARY 22, 1931: Sister Faustina sees the Lord Jesus dressed in a white robe. Red and pale rays stream forth from the area of His Heart. **Paint an image, He tells her, according to the pattern you see, bearing the signature, "Jesus, I trust in You."**

JANUARY 2, 1934: Sister Faustina meets with the artist Eugene Kazimirowski, who, through Fr. Michael Sopocko (her spiritual director and confessor), has been commissioned to paint the image of The Divine Mercy.

JUNE 1934: The Kazimirowski painting is completed. Sister Faustina is disappointed with it and cries to the Lord, "Who will paint You as beautiful as You are?" In reply, she hears the words, **Not in the beauty of the color nor of the brush lies the greatness of this image, but in My grace** (*Diary*, 313). The painting is hung in the corridor of the Bernardine Sisters' Convent near St. Michael's Church in Vilnius, where Fr. Sopocko is rector.

JULY 1934: Following the instructions of her spiritual director (Fr. Sopocko), Sr. Faustina begins keeping a personal diary, which she entitles *Divine Mercy in My Soul.*

AUGUST 1934: Sister Faustina suffers a violent attack of asthma for the first time, perhaps already due to tuberculosis, which is to cause her almost constant suffering for the few remaining years of her life.

OCTOBER 26, 1934: Sister Faustina sees the Lord Jesus above the chapel in Vilnius, with the same red and pale rays coming from the area of His Heart. The rays envelop the chapel and the students' infirmary, and then spread out over the whole world.

APRIL 26-28, 1935: During the celebration concluding the Jubilee Year of the Redemption of the world, the Kazimirowski image of The Divine Mercy is transferred to Ostra Brama (Shrine of Our Lady of Mercy in Vilnius) and placed in a high window so it may be seen from far away. This event coincides with the Second Sunday of Easter, which, according to Sister Faustina, is to be celebrated as the Feast of Divine Mercy. Father Sopocko delivers a homily about The Divine Mercy.

JANUARY 8, 1936: Sister Faustina visits Bishop Romuald Jalbrzykowski and tells him that Jesus has asked for a new congregation to be founded.

OCTOBER 5, 1936: Father Sopocko writes to Sr. Faustina, asking for the texts of the Chaplet and the Novena to The Divine Mercy.

DECEMBER 9, 1936: With her health deteriorating, Sr. Faustina is sent to the hospital in Pradnik, a sanatorium in Krakow for tuberculosis patients. Except for a few days during the Christmas season, she remains there until March 27, 1937.

DECEMBER 13, 1936: Under the appearance of her confessor, Jesus Himself hears Sr. Faustina's confession.

APRIL 4, 1937: Father Sopocko publishes an article on The Divine Mercy in the *Vilnius Catholic Weekly*.

APRIL 4, 1937: By permission of Archbishop Romuald Jalbrzykowski, the Kazmirowski image is blessed and placed in St. Michael's Church in Vilnius.

SEPTEMBER 27, 1937: Sister Faustina and Mother Irene meet with the printer who is to print holy cards bearing the image of The Divine Mercy.

NOVEMBER 1937: Through the efforts of Fr. Sopocko, the Litany, Chaplet, and Novena to The Divine Mercy are published by the J. Cebulski Press in Krakow in a pamphlet entitled "Christ, King of Mercy." On the cover of the pamphlet is a color picture representing the merciful Christ with the signature, "Jesus, I trust in You." Holy cards, bearing a copy of Kazimirowski's image of The Divine Mercy on the front, and the chaplet on the back, are also printed by Cebulski.

NOVEMBER 10, 1937: Sister Faustina and Mother Superior Irene look over the pamphlet containing the Litany, Chaplet, and Novena, to The Divine Mercy, and the Lord tells Sr.

Faustina that many souls have already been drawn to Him through the image.

APRIL 21, 1938: Suffering greatly from tuberculosis, Sr. Faustina leaves the convent for her final, five-month stay at the sanatorium in Pradnik.

APRIL 22-MAY 6, 1938: For 14 days, at the sanatorium in Pradnik, Sr. Faustina receives Holy Communion from an angel.

JUNE 24, 1938: Sister Faustina sees the Sacred Heart of Jesus in the sky in the midst of a great brilliance. Rays are streaming from the wound in His side and spreading out over the entire world.

JUNE 1938: She stops writing the *Diary* due to illness.

SEPTEMBER 2, 1938: Father Sopocko visits her at the sanatorium in Pradnik and discovers her in ecstasy.

SEPTEMBER 26, 1938: Father Sopocko visits her in Krakow for the last time and notes that "she looked like an unearthly being, ... I no longer had the slightest doubt that what she had written in her *Diary* about receiving Holy Communion from an angel was really true."

OCTOBER 5, 1938: At 10:45 p.m., Sr. Faustina dies of multiple tuberculosis in Krakow, at the age of 33.

OCTOBER 7, 1938: Her funeral coincides with the First Friday of the month and the Feast of Our Lady of the Rosary.

SEPTEMBER 1, 1939: German tanks and planes cross the Polish frontier, and the Nazis take control of Poland. In the course of the war, the city of Warsaw, along with many other Polish cities and towns, is destroyed by incendiary and demolition bombs, an apparent fulfillment of Sr. Faustina's earlier prophecy:

> One day Jesus told me that He would cause a chastise-ment to fall upon the most beautiful city in our country [probably, Warsaw]. This chastisement would be that

with which God had punished Sodom and Gomorrah (*Diary*, 39).

SPRING, 1940: Father Joseph Jarzebowski, MIC, a Marian priest from Warsaw who had been blacklisted by the Nazi SS, hears about the devotion to The Divine Mercy at a camp in Vikomir, Lithuania.

JULY-SEPTEMBER 1940: Father Jarzebowski prays to The Divine Mercy to help him escape to America.

FEBRUARY 25, 1941: Hearing of Fr. Jarzebowski's plan to escape, Fr. Sopocko gives him a Latin memorandum outlining the message and devotion to The Divine Mercy. Father Jarzebowski promises to do his best to keep the memorandum safe and have it printed when he reaches America. Entrusting himself and his mission to The Divine Mercy, he vows to spend the rest of his life spreading the mercy message and devotion if he reaches safety.

FEBRUARY 26, 1941: Carrying a picture of the merciful Jesus next to his heart and Fr. Sopocko's Divine Mercy memorandum in his traveling bag, Fr. Jarzebowski leaves his hiding place in Vilnius and boards an ordinary trans-Siberian train. Traveling across the whole of Russia and Siberia, he reaches Vladivostock, where the customs officer searches everything except the bag containing the memorandum. No one seems to notice that his American visa is obsolete and invalid, and he is granted Japanese transit.

When he reaches Japan, he finds $30.00 and a ticket to the United States waiting for him, sent by Fr. Joseph Luniewski, MIC, of the Marians in America. The Polish embassy validates his American visa, and he leaves for the United States.

MAY 1941: Father Jarzebowski lands on American soil. Full of gratitude to the mercy of God and remembering his promises to Fr. Sopocko, he begins to share the message and devotion of mercy privately. At a Detroit print shop, the first sample copies of the image are made.

JUNE 1941: Asked to assist as confessor at the annual retreat for the Felician Sisters in Enfield, Connecticut, Fr. Jarzebowski speaks to the sisters about the revelations to Sr. Faustina and the essence of the message and devotion to The Divine Mercy, mentioning the special graces given to him. The sisters make a copy of his brief account, and the provincial superior donates a sum of money to have several hundred copies of the image printed.

1941: At a "house meeting" in Washington, D.C., a tiny group of Marians decides to undertake as an apostolate the spreading of the message and devotion to The Divine Mercy, and they begin printing the first novena leaflets.

NOVEMBER 28, 1958: Sister Faustina's prophecy about the apparent destruction of the devotion to The Divine Mercy (see *Diary*, 378 and 1659) begins its fulfillment by a decree of condemnation due to incorrect translations in the Italian version of her *Diary*. The severe ban is mitigated by Pope John XXIII on March 6, 1959, to a "Notification" that prohibited "the spreading of the devotion according to Sr. Faustina."

OCTOBER 21, 1965: In the Archdiocese of Krakow, 27 years after the death of Faustina, Bishop Julian Groblicki, specially delegated by Archbishop Karol Wojtyla, begins the Informative Process relating to the life and virtues of Sr. Faustina. From this moment, Sr. Faustina is worthy of the title "Servant of God."

NOVEMBER 25, 1966: While the Informative Process relating to the virtues, writings, and devotion of the Servant of God Sr. Faustina is being conducted (October 21, 1965, to September 20, 1967), her remains are exhumed and translated to a tomb specially prepared for this purpose in the chapel of the Sisters of Our Lady of Mercy in Lagiewniki. Over the tomb is a black slab with a cross in the center. The slab usually has fresh flowers brought by the faithful, who plead for numerous graces through her intercession.

JUNE 26, 1967: Archbishop Karol Wojtyla becomes Cardinal Karol Wojtyla.

SEPTEMBER 20, 1967: The Archbishop of Krakow, Cardinal Karol Wojtyla, officially closes the first informative stage in the process for the beatification of the Servant of God Sr. Faustina Kowalska.

JANUARY 31, 1968: By a decree of the Sacred Congregation for the Causes of Saints, the Process of Beatification of the Servant of God Sr. Faustina Kowalska is formally inaugurated.

APRIL 15, 1978: In response to inquiries from Poland, and in particular Cardinal Wojtyla, about the "Notification" of 1959, the Sacred Congregation for the Canonization of Saints declares the Notification is no longer binding due to the changed circumstances and the opinion of many Polish ordinaries.

OCTOBER 16, 1978: Cardinal Karol Wojtyla is elected Pope John Paul II.

NOVEMBER 30, 1980: Pope John Paul II publishes his encyclical letter *Rich in Mercy* (*Dives in Misericordia*), in which he stresses that Jesus Christ has revealed God, who is "rich in mercy," as the Father. He speaks of mercy as "the most stupendous attribute of the Creator and Redeemer" (RIM, 13).

JUNE 19, 1981: The Sacred Congregation for the Causes of Saints, having completed the investigation of all available writings of the Servant of God Sr. Faustina, issues a decree stating that "nothing stands in the way of proceeding further" with her cause.

OCTOBER 8, 1981: The Sacred Congregation for the Sacraments and Divine Worship issues a decree confirming the Latin text of a Votive Mass of The Divine Mercy for the Metropolitan Archdiocese of Krakow, Poland.

APRIL 10, 1991: Pope John Paul II, at his general audience, speaks about Sr. Faustina, showing his great respect for her, relating her to his encyclical *Rich in Mercy*, and emphasizing her role in bringing the message of mercy to the world.

MARCH 7, 1992: In the presence of the Holy Father, the Congregation for the Causes of Saints promulgates the Decree of Heroic Virtues, by which the Church acknowledges that Sr. Faustina practiced all the Christian virtues to a heroic degree. As a result, she receives the title "Venerable" Servant of God, and the way is opened for verification of the miracle attributed to her intercession.

In that same year, the healing of Maureen Digan at the tomb of Sr. Faustina is recognized as a miracle by three separate panels appointed by the Sacred Congregation: first a panel of doctors, then of theologians, and finally, of cardinals and bishops.

DECEMBER 21, 1992: The Holy Father publishes the Church's acceptance of the miracle as granted through the intercession of Sr. Faustina and announces the date for her solemn beatification.

APRIL 18, 1993: St. Faustina is beatified in Rome on the Second Sunday of Easter (which our Lord has revealed to her as the "Feast of Divine Mercy").

SEPTEMBER 4, 1993: John Paul II prays the Rosary at the Shrine of Our Lady of Mercy, Ostra Brama, in Vilnius, Lithuania, where the image of the Merciful Jesus was first displayed.

SEPTEMBER 5, 1993: John Paul II kneels and prays before the image of The Divine Mercy, painted under the direction of Sr. Faustina, in the Church of the Holy Spirit, Vilnius.

JANUARY 23, 1995: Pope John Paul II grants to the Polish Bishops that the Sunday after Easter be the Sunday of Divine Mercy because of the need and desire of the faithful.

APRIL 23, 1995: Pope John Paul II celebrates Divine Mercy Sunday in Holy Spirit Church, the Shrine of The Divine Mercy in Rome (*L'Osservatore Romano*, English Edition, April 26, 1995). In his homily, he challenges us to "trust in the Lord and be apostles of Divine Mercy."

In his *"Regina Caeli"* address, he speaks of this Sunday as the day of thanksgiving for God's mercy, called the Sunday of Divine Mercy. He challenges us to personally experience this mercy in order to be merciful and forgive — and so "break the spiral of violence by the *miracle of forgiveness*" (emphasis in original).

JUNE 7, 1997: Pope John Paul II makes a pilgrimage to the Shrine of The Divine Mercy in Lagiewniki (Krakow), Poland, at the convent where the relics of Sr. Faustina are honored. He says, "The message of Divine Mercy has always been near and dear to me." John Paul II then goes on to highlight how Divine Mercy helped him and his compatriots in Poland endure "the tragic experience of the Second World War," emphasizing, "This was also my personal experience, which I took with me to the See of Peter and which in a sense forms the image of this Pontificate."

NOVEMBER 20, 1999: Pope John Paul II accepts the healing of the heart of Fr. Ronald Pytel of Baltimore, Maryland, as the miracle for the canonization of then Blessed Faustina.

APRIL 30, 2000: Pope John Paul II canonizes Sr. Faustina Kowalska and proclaims Divine Mercy Sunday for the universal Church. The canonization occurs on Divine Mercy Sunday and is held in St. Peter's Square in Rome. In his homily, he repeats three times that Sr. Faustina is "God's gift to our time." He also passes on the message of Divine Mercy to the new millennium. Of Divine Mercy Sunday, he says in his homily, "It is important that we accept the whole message that comes to us in the Word of God on this Second Sunday of Easter, which from now on throughout the Church will be called 'Divine Mercy Sunday.'"

APRIL 17, 2002: Pope John Paul II consecrates the Basilica of The Divine Mercy in Krakow-Lagiewniki, Poland, and entrusts the World to Divine Mercy. Before he solemnly entrusts the world to Divine Mercy, Pope John Paul says, "I do so with the burning desire that the message of God's merciful love, proclaimed here through St. Faustina, *may be made known to all the peoples of the earth* and fill their hearts with hope" (emphasis in original).

APRIL 2, 2005: Pope John Paul II dies on the Vigil of Divine Mercy Sunday. It is altogether fitting that the Great Mercy Pope who established Divine Mercy Sunday for the universal Church goes home to God on its vigil. He leaves his last annual Divine Mercy Sunday message, which is shared with the faithful in St. Peter's Square on April 3, Divine Mercy Sunday. He closes his message with this summary of The Divine Mercy message and devotion: "Jesus, I trust in You, have mercy upon us and upon the whole world. Amen."

APRIL 19, 2005: Cardinal Joseph Ratzinger is elected Pope and chooses the name of Benedict XVI. In his first message as Pope on April 20, Benedict XVI expresses "deep gratitude for a gift of Divine Mercy." He says that he considers it "a special grace" obtained for him by his predecessor, John Paul II. He goes on to say of John Paul, "I seem to feel his strong hand clasping mine; I seem to see his smiling eyes and hear his words, at this moment addressed specifically to me, 'Do not be afraid!'"

MAY 2006: Pope Benedict XVI goes on pilgrimage to Poland, the homeland of John Paul II. On his pilgrimage, Pope Benedict visits the International Shrine of The Divine Mercy in Lagiewniki, Poland. He says in his general audience of May 31 of his visit there:

> It was here in the neighboring convent that Sr. Faustina Kowalska, contemplating the shining wounds of the Risen Christ, received a message of trust for humanity which John Paul II echoed and interpreted and which really is a central message precisely for our time: Mercy as God's power, as a barrier against the evil of the world.

APRIL 2-6, 2008: The first World Apostolic Congress on Mercy is held in the Vatican. More than 4,000 participants comprising some 200 delegations from every corner of the globe convene in Rome on April 2 for the first World Apostolic Congress on Mercy. Pope Benedict XVI inaugurates the Congress by celebrating Holy Mass in St. Peter's Square on April 2, the third anniversary of the death of John Paul II. In his homily, Pope Benedict underscores John Paul II's legacy of mercy and St. Faustina as "a prophetic messenger of Divine Mercy" for John Paul in helping him make sense of the "terrible tragedies of the 20th century." The plenary sessions for the Congress are held in St. John Lateran Basilica, the cathedral of the Bishop of Rome, and many prominent cardinals and bishops attend the sessions. Then, at the conclusion of the Congress, on April 6, Pope Benedict gives his Divine Mercy mandate in his *Regina Caeli* message:

> Yes, dear friends, the first World Congress on Divine Mercy ended this morning. ... I thank the organizers, especially the Vicariate of Rome, and to all the participants I address my cordial greeting which now becomes a mandate: *go forth and be witnesses of God's mercy*, a source of hope for every person and for the whole world. May the Risen Lord be with you always! (emphasis added).

SEPTEMBER 28, 2008: The spiritual director and confessor of St. Faustina, Fr. Michael Sopocko, is beatified in Bialystok, Poland, with an estimated 70,000 people attending. They include 100 religious sisters from 13 countries representing the Congregation of the Sisters of the Merciful Jesus, an order founded by Blessed Michael. Pope Benedict XVI addresses the assembly live by satellite feed from Castel Gandolfo, Italy, and says of Blessed Michael:

> At his suggestion, [Sister] Faustina described her mystical experiences and apparitions of the merciful Jesus in her well-known *Diary*. Thanks to his efforts,

the image with the words, "Jesus, I trust in You" was painted and transmitted to the world. The Servant of God became known as a zealous priest, teacher, and promoter of the Divine Mercy devotion. ... My beloved Predecessor, the Servant of God John Paul II most certainly rejoices in this beatification in the Father's house.

MARIAN PRESS

STOCKBRIDGE, MA

Your Trustworthy Resource for Publications on Divine Mercy and Mary

PROMOTING DIVINE MERCY SINCE 1941

Marian Press, the publishing apostolate of the Marian Fathers of the Immaculate Conception of the B.V.M., has published and distributed millions of religious books, magazines, and pamphlets that teach, encourage, and edify Catholics around the world. Our publications promote and support the ministry and spirituality of the Marians worldwide. Loyal to the Holy Father and to the teachings of the Catholic Church, the Marians fulfill their special mission by:

- Fostering devotion to Mary, the Immaculate Conception.

- Promoting The Divine Mercy message and devotion.

- Offering assistance to the dying and the deceased, especially the victims of war and disease.

- Promoting Christian knowledge, administering parishes and shrines, and conducting missions.

Based in Stockbridge, Mass., Marian Press is known as the publisher of the *Diary of Saint Maria Faustina Kowalska*, and the Marians are the leading authorities on The Divine Mercy message and devotion.

Stockbridge is also the home of the National Shrine of The Divine Mercy, the Association of Marian Helpers, and a destination for thousands of pilgrims each year.

Globally, the Marians' ministries also include missions in developing countries where the spiritual and material needs are enormous.

To learn more about the Marians, their spirituality, publications or ministries, visit **marian.org** or **thedivinemercy.org**, the Marians' website that is devoted exclusively to Divine Mercy.

Below is a view of the National Shrine of The Divine Mercy and its Residence in Stockbridge, Mass. The Shrine, which was built in the 1950s, was declared a National Shrine by the National Conference of Catholic Bishops on March 20, 1996.

© MARIE ROMAGNANO

OTHER BOOKS BY FR. KOSICKI

Based on the *Diary of St. Faustina*, these perpetual devotionals are beautifully compiled by thematic topics and follow a generic calendar — so readers can start using them any day of any year.

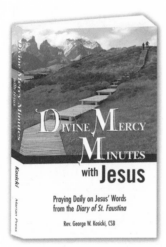

DIVINE MERCY MINUTES WITH JESUS focuses on the words of Jesus in the *Diary* — exemplifying the key elements of The Divine Mercy message. The compiler, Fr. George Kosicki, CSB, includes a daily prayer response to help you grow in your personal relationship with the Merciful Savior.

MMWJ 9781596141933

For those who love Saint Faustina, **MERCY MINUTES: DAILY GEMS OF ST. FAUSTINA ...** will help you grow each day as an apostle of Divine Mercy through astounding insights into the saint's spirituality. This revised edition of the bestselling devotional features a foreword by Fr. Joseph Roesch, MIC, a well-known face on EWTN Global Network, as well as a special dedication to Pope Benedict XVI for his participation at the first World Apostolic Congress on Mercy, held in Rome in 2008.

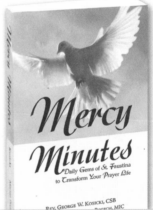

MMIN2 9781596142008

ESSENTIAL DIVINE MERCY RESOURCES

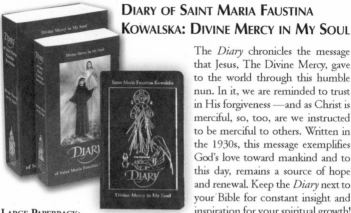

DIARY OF SAINT MARIA FAUSTINA KOWALSKA: DIVINE MERCY IN MY SOUL

The *Diary* chronicles the message that Jesus, The Divine Mercy, gave to the world through this humble nun. In it, we are reminded to trust in His forgiveness —and as Christ is merciful, so, too, are we instructed to be merciful to others. Written in the 1930s, this message exemplifies God's love toward mankind and to this day, remains a source of hope and renewal. Keep the *Diary* next to your Bible for constant insight and inspiration for your spiritual growth!

LARGE PAPERBACK:
NBFD 9780944203040
768 pages, including 24 pages of color photographs, 5 ¼" x 7 ¾".

COMPACT PAPERBACK:
DNBF 9781596141100
768 pages, including 24 pages of black and white photographs, 4" x 7".

DELUXE LEATHER-BOUND EDITION

Treasure this handsome, Deluxe Leather Edition for years to come. Includes a special dedication from the Marians of the Immaculate Conception in commemoration of the first World Apostolic Congress on Mercy, gilded edges, a ribbon marker, and 20 pages of color photographs.768 pages, 4 ⅜" x 7 ⅛".

BURGUNDY: DDBURG **9781596141896**
NAVY BLUE: DDBLUE **9781596141902**

FAUSTINA: SAINT FOR OUR TIMES
by Fr. George W. Kosicki, CSB

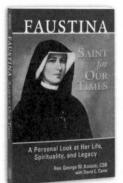

This is more than a biography or a historical presentation of a life once lived. Through years of studying her *Diary* and immersing himself in Divine Mercy, Fr. George W. Kosicki, CSB, came to know St. Faustina — not as some remote visionary but as a real person, fulfilling her promise to return to earth to encourage others to trust in God's mercy (see *Diary*, 1582).

"I rejoice in this book! Discover why Pope John Paul II called St. Faustina 'a gift of God to our time.' May she become for you — as she is for Fr. Kosicki — a sister who will walk with you, intercede for you, and teach you what it means to live in the mercy of God."

— Vinny Flynn
Author, *7 Secrets of the Eucharist*

STF 9781596142268

ESSENTIAL DIVINE MERCY RESOURCES

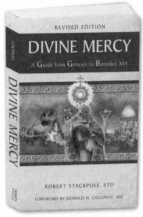

AGGB2   9781596142084

DIVINE MERCY: A GUIDE FROM GENESIS TO BENEDICT XVI

"This is a book that disciples of Divine Mercy have been waiting for! It's a guide to what Scripture, the Church's great theologians, the saints, and recent popes have said about Divine Mercy. I highly recommend it."

> — Fr. Benedict Groeschel, CFR
> EWTN TV Host

Revised edition includes more on St. Augustine and Pope Benedict XVI, as well as a new chapter on St. Bernard of Clairvaux. Written by Robert Stackpole, STD. Foreword by Fr. Donald H. Calloway, MIC.

DISCOVER THE MANDATE

Pope Benedict's Divine Mercy Mandate is brilliantly written. David Came traces the thread of Divine Mercy throughout the papacy of Benedict XVI and pulls back the veil on a papal program for what it means to "go forth and be witnesses of God's mercy." This is a must-read.

> — Drew Mariani, Nationally syndicated radio talk show host, author, and award-winning journalist

PBBK   9781596142039

THE DIVINE MERCY MESSAGE AND DEVOTION

Fr. Seraphim Michalenko, MIC, with Vinny Flynn and Robert A. Stackpole.

Outlining The Divine Mercy message and devotion in an easy-to-follow format, this booklet provides an overview to one of the Catholic Church's fastest growing movements. Includes all elements and essential prayers of The Divine Mercy message and devotion.

M17   9780944203583

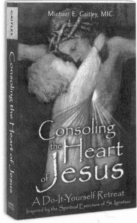